GW00857867

SEX: HOW? WHY? WHAT

SEX: HOW? WHY? WHAT?

THE TEENAGER'S GUIDE

by Jane Goldman

PICCADILLY PRESS • LONDON

This book is dedicated with lots of love and a thousand thank yous to my unfeasibly perfect family - Jonathan, Betty, Harvey, Amanda, Stuart, Kinny and Bunker.

Thanks also to the lovely Jacqui Deevoy for her help with this book.

Printed and bound by The Bath Press
for the publishers, Piccadilly Press Ltd.,
5 Castle Road, London NW1 8PR

A catalogue record for this book is available from the British Library.

ISBN: 1 85340 213 3 (Hardback)
1 85340 218 4 (Trade paperback)

Jane Goldman was born in 1970. She lives in North London with her husband and two children. She worked for a number of years for *Just Seventeen* magazine and is now a freelance journalist and writer. This is her second book. Her first, *Thirteensomething*, was also published by Piccadilly Press.

CONTENTS

INTRODUCTION

Sex is a very natural thing. After all, humans are born with all the body bits they need to have sex, and most people get the urge to use them at some point in their lives – whether it's to make a baby, to show their love for someone, or just because it feels fabulous.

We're pretty sexual creatures right from the minute we're born. Even babies touch their private parts because it feels nice, and if you think about it, little kids' games like doctors and nurses often involve a fair bit of crafty groping. And once you hit your teenage years, sex is likely to be in your thoughts one heck of a lot. The point is that sexual stuff comes naturally to us, and there's nothing wrong with enjoying your own body – it's as normal a part of being a living creature as eating, sleeping and going to the loo. Back in the days when we all lived in caves, playing with yourself or having sex were probably about as much of a big deal as those other bodily functions. Several thousand years on, however, sex has become a very complicated issue indeed. The mere fact that this book even exists proves the point – after all, when did you last see a book about how to go to the loo? Or hear politicians arguing about what age kids should start being taught about the ins and outs of sleeping? Sex is no longer just a bodily function, but a jolly big deal. It all comes down to centuries of changing attitudes about sex and our bodies, not to mention the fact that these days we have all sorts of things to worry about like unwanted pregnancies and sexually transmitted diseases, including AIDS. This means that we not only have a truckload of questions and worries, but also a feeling of embarrassment and confusion about sexual things which makes it really hard to ask our questions and put our minds at rest. What a mess, eh?

No one can change the way the world is today, but everyone can change what goes on in their own lives. Hopefully, reading this book will be a big step towards doing that. In it, you'll find everything you need to know about how your body works, how other people's bodies work and what sex is all about. You'll also find the answers to lots and lots of questions. Most of us fret about the same things (which is quite reassuring in itself, isn't it?), so hopefully some of the questions will be the very same ones that have popped into your head and started bugging you, or might pop into your head in the future.

Hopefully, reading this book will be a big step towards making your experiences of sex safe and unconfusing — not to mention wonderful, heavenly and fun. Sadly, no book can claim to unravel the mysteries of love. Even those huge, American "relationship psychology" books with preposterous, long titles can't *promise* to make anyone's personal life go smoothly.

Nope, dealing with the love part is *your* job. Of course, you don't have to be in love to have sex, but remember that true love and good sex are two of the greatest pleasures on the planet. Experiencing both at the same time is about as near perfect as life can get.

Chapter One

Your Body

When you're a little kid, you don't really give your body that much thought. Then along comes puberty and — bang! — that great, relaxed attitude you had goes right out the window. It's bye-bye to peace-of-mind and hello to hours of wondering, worrying and wiggling yourself into odd positions in front of the mirror to get a better look. (Not to mention all the other new and alien things which don't begin with W!)

Puberty is the proper word for the time in your life when your body changes from a kid's body into an adult's body. It's a vaguely amusing word (possibly because it has the word pube in it), but puberty itself isn't terribly amusing at all. Weird — yes, surprising — yes, scary — sometimes.

Embarrassing? Wonderful? Horrible? Exciting? Yes, puberty is indeed all these things and much, much more. But amusing? Sadly not, unless it's all happening to someone else and you have a spectacularly childish sense of humour, in which case it's downright hilarious. With light relief in such short supply, puberty can be a tricky time. The best way to cope is to take it easy and keep on top of what's going on by being smart, aware and totally well-informed. And what better place to start getting clued-up than right here?

GETTING TO KNOW YOUR BODY

Okay, so you know that boys' and girls' bodies are pretty different right from the word go. Let's check out exactly who's got what, and where...

Boys

If you're a boy, you're probably already well aquainted with your main bit of apparatus — the penis. *Willy, cock, knob, dick, prick, tool, todger, tackle* and *John Thomas* are just a few of the weird and wonderful nicknames for it. Your penis is made of soft body tissue, chock full of blood vessels. When you get sexually excited, blood rushes into the vessels, and a ring of muscles at the base of the penis tightens to stop the blood flowing out again. The result is that your willy gets bigger and harder and can stand up all by itself. This is called getting an erection — or in slang terms, a *hard-on, stiffy* or *stonker.* Taking a closer look, your willy is made up of two sections: the *shaft* (the long bit) and the *head,* or *glans* (the bobbly bit on top). The head has tons of nerve endings in it, which is why it feels extra-nice when you touch it. The head is covered and protected by a moveable bit of skin called a *foreskin,* although you might have had yours removed for religious or medical reasons. This is called being *circumcised.*

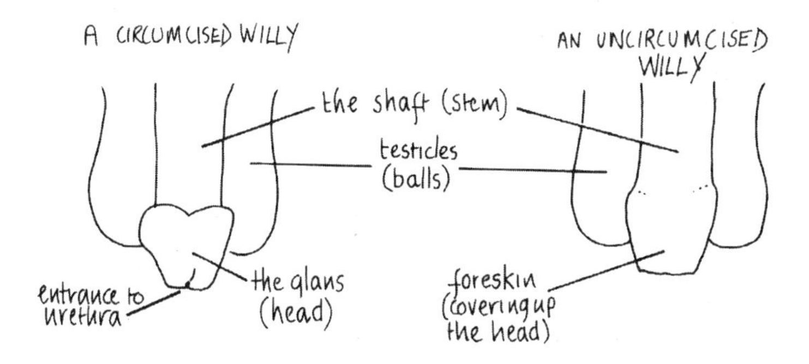

Underneath your willy are your *testicles* or *testes* (also called *balls, bollocks, nuts, cobblers*). These two little round organs are snuggled inside a kind of skin bag, called the *scrotal sac* or *scrotum,* and they store *sperm* — the weeny little living cells which have the potential to make a baby. When you're warm and relaxed, the scrotum looks soft and you can clearly see the shape of the balls inside. When you're tense, sexually excited or just a bit chilly, the whole thing gets much firmer and pulls itself up closer to your body in a neat, crinkly-looking little package.

There's lots going on inside your body, too. The little hole at the end of your willy is the entrance to a tube called the *urethra* which does two jobs. Firstly, it leads from your bladder and lets your wee out. Secondly, it joins up with the tube which comes from your internal sex organs, where your sperm and something else called *semen* is made. Semen (also known as *spunk, cum, jism* and *juice*) is a sticky, whitish liquid. It gets mixed up with all the incy-wincy little sperm, which are too small to be seen by the human eye, and therefore need to be kept safely under control!

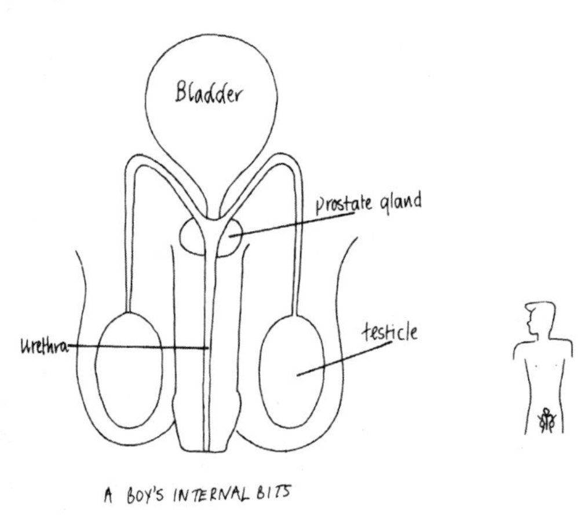

A BOY'S INTERNAL BITS

When you play with yourself, have sex or even have a sexy dream, and you reach a point where you can't get any more sexually excited, you have an *orgasm* — a great, big, lovely, rushing feeling of excitement, and that's when *ejaculation* happens. This means that a batch of the sperm and semen you've been storing up comes spurting out of the end of your willy. This is also known as *coming, climaxing, shooting your load* and *blowing your wad.*

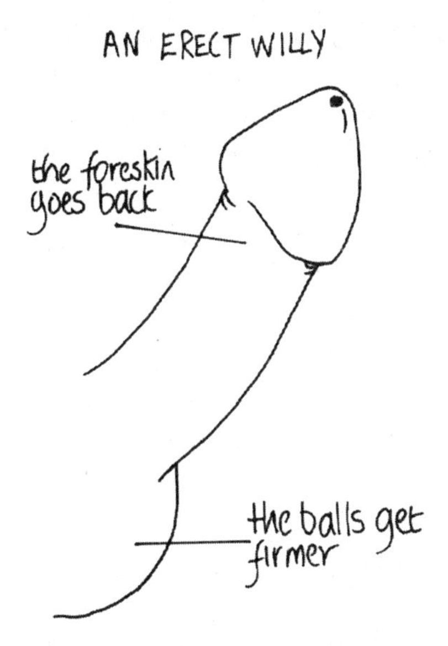

All of a boy's most important sexual equipment is below his belt. It's worth noting, however, that you've also got two nipples. Unlike a girl's nipples (which work as outlets for milk when she has a baby), yours don't serve any particular function. They *do* have a bunch of nerve endings in them, though. This means that it can feel good when they're touched, and you might notice that they go hard if you squeeze, rub or stroke them.

Girls

Unlike a boy, a girl has most of her important bits tucked away inside her. Your *vagina* is a passage which starts with an opening between your legs and ends a few inches up, at the entrance to your womb, which is called the *cervix.* There aren't as many nicknames for vaginas as there are for willies, but there are still quite a few, like *fanny, hole, quim, snatch, pussy* or *twat. Cunt* is another one, but it's also quite a strong swear word that people use as an insult, so many girls feel that it's not a great name to use for such a nice part of their body! Your vagina is a very versatile thing: it lets a willy in during sex, lets your periods out, and is also the route

A GIRL'S INTERNAL-BITS

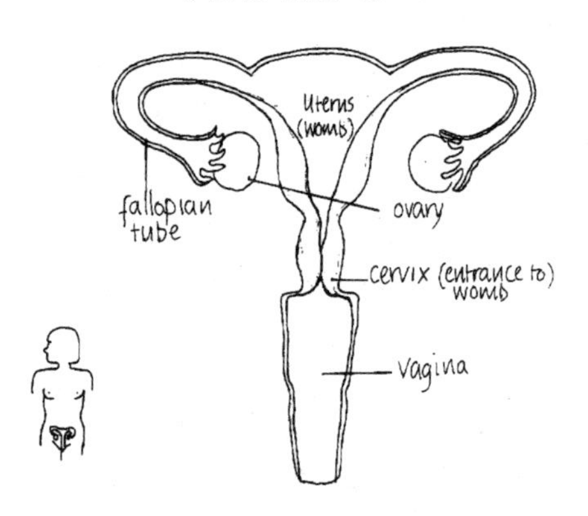

that your babies will take from your womb to the outside world, if you decide to have any. If you have a closer look between your legs, you might find that the entrance is covered by a thin film of skin called a hymen (see Chapter Four for more about it).

Inside, you've also got two *ovaries,* where your body stores eggs (which have the potential to make babies), and two tunnels called *Fallopian tubes* for the eggs to travel down when they're ripe.

There's plenty going on outside your body too. Firstly, there's what's called the *mound of Venus* — the soft bump of flesh over your pubic bone, where your pubic hair grows. Moving down-under, everything is more hidden away, but if you take a close look, you'll find that on either side of the entrance to your vagina are a pair of little lips (called the *labia minora*), and a pair of bigger, outer lips (*the labia majora*). Directly above all that is a tiny little hole which is the entrance to your *urethra* — the tube that leads from your bladder. This is where your wee comes out. Right at the top of the whole caboodle is a delicate little bump, protected by a little hood of skin. This is your *clitoris* (some people call it *clit* for short), a neat bundle of nerve endings. It's a very interesting and important bit of you, because its only reason for being there is to make you feel nice, sexually, when it gets touched.

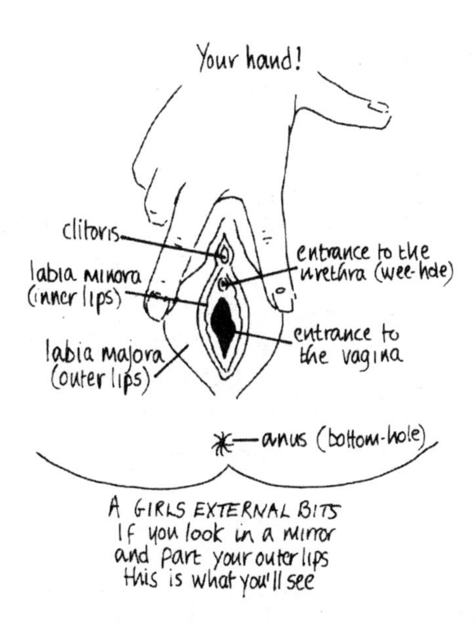

A GIRLS EXTERNAL BITS
If you look in a mirror and part your outer lips this is what you'll see

Although your clitoris feels and looks just like a little bump, about the size of a very, very small pea, it's actually a bit like a tiny willy, made up of a *shaft* and a *head.* Like a willy, blood rushes into it when you get sexually excited, making it go hard — though you wouldn't necessarily notice this happening. When your clitoris is touched, the excitement builds up, and often ends with an *orgasm.* Unlike boys, girls don't get anything spurting out of them when this happens — it just feels mega-nice. (See Chapter Two for more info.)

Moving higher up your body, you'll find your *breasts* — also called *bosoms, boobs, tits, titties, knockers* and about a million other names. If you haven't gone through puberty yet, you'll just find your nipples. Inside, behind them, are all sorts of clever milk-making glands so that you can breastfeed your baby if you want to, but that's not the only reason you have bosoms. They're also there to give you sexual pleasure, thanks to lots of sensitive nerve endings, especially in the nipples.

PUBERTY — WHAT'S THE DEAL?

Throughout this book, you're bound to notice that we keep coming back to one particular fact: everyone is different. The puberty situation is no exception — everyone hits puberty at different times. For boys, we're looking at some point between the ages of ten and sixteen. For girls, it's between nine and fifteen. Everyone's puberty follows a different pattern, too — the changes can happen dead fast and all at once, or pretty slowly, spaced out over a number of years. Whatever, most people find that their puberty is all over and done with by the time they're seventeen (girls) or eighteen (boys). If you started early, you could finish much earlier. Having said that, some changes can go on happening right up until your mid-20s — for instance, boys' bodies and faces can get hairier, and girls' bosoms can get bigger.

Despite the differences in *when* puberty happens, *what* happens is much the same for everyone. Here's what you can expect:

Boys

- Your willy and balls will get slightly bigger.

- You'll get hard-ons more often, sometimes when you'd least expect it!

- You might experience "wet dreams" - having an exciting, sexy dream, then waking up to find that you've come in your sleep. (The boring, sensible word for these is *nocturnal emissions.*) You may not remember the dream or the orgasm, but you'll probably notice a damp patch on your night-clothes or on the bed, where you ejaculated.

• You'll grow extra body-hair, especially under your armpits and near your tackle. The hair above and around your willy and balls is called *pubic hair* (aka pubes), and it's usually darker, coarser and curlier than the hair you've got elsewhere.

• Your skin might get greasier, so you'll be more prone to getting spots than before.

• Your hair might get greasier and need washing more often.

• You'll sweat more, especially under your armpits, and you may notice that your sweat smells stronger than it used to. Although fresh sweat smells fine, stale sweat pongs something rotten, so if you don't wash regularly and use a deodorant, you'll get pretty stinky.

• You'll get taller, often in a madly quick growing spurt.

• You'll put on weight. This doesn't mean you'll get fat — just that your body will fill out into a more adult shape.

• You'll get stronger.

• Your voice will "break". This means that eventually it'll be deeper and lower — a man's voice rather than a boy's. Some boys simply wake up one morning to find they've got a new voice, but for others the change can be slower and weirder — you could go through a period where your voice wobbles alarmingly between being high and low, with the odd mysterious squeak and croak coming out now and then!

• You might get some hair on your chest — although some men never do.

• You'll get hair on your face.

GIRLS

• Your nipples will grow bigger and maybe get a little darker.

• You'll grow bosoms. They might start off feeling like lumps. You might notice a tingly feeling or even "growing pains" as they develop, and find that they suddenly become very sensitive — accidentally getting elbowed in the boob at this stage can make you see stars!

• The little lips on either side of your fanny get fuller, but you probably won't notice the change.

• You'll discover the odd bit of white gooey stuff in your pants. This is called *discharge*, it comes out of your fanny, and it's just a sign that everything inside is working properly.

- You'll grow pubic hair above and around your privates, which will probably be darker, coarser and curlier than hair you've got elsewhere.

- You'll grow hair under your armpits.

- The hair on your legs will get slightly darker and thicker — and therefore more noticeable.

- You might get the odd hair (or a whole bunch) growing where you didn't expect it — such as around your nipples, on your tummy or even on your face, around your chin or upper-lip.

- Your skin might get greasier, so you'll be more prone to getting spots than before.

- Your hair might get greasier and need washing more often.

- Your armpits will sweat more and smell stronger, so you'll need to wash a lot and use a deodorant to keep yourself smelling sweet.

- You'll put on weight, and your body will probably fill out into a more adult shape, with curvier hips and a more pronounced waist.

- You'll get stronger.

- Your voice will get a bit lower and deeper, but you

probably won't notice it happening.

• You'll start having periods...

PERIODS

Here's the low-down:
• The medical term for periods is *menstruation*. Slang terms for them include *coming on, time of the month, being on the rag, having the painters in* and *getting the curse.*

• This is what happens when you get a period: One of your ovaries releases a ripe egg (this is called *ovulation*). The egg travels down the Fallopian tube towards your womb. Your womb makes a special, thick lining just in case the egg meets a sperm, gets fertilised by it, and needs a safe, comfortable place for a baby to grow. If the egg doesn't meet any sperm, your body knows that there isn't going to be a baby, so it gets rid of the lining, along with the egg and a bit of blood.

• You'll know for sure when you get your first period because you'll find blood in your pants. It can be bright red, like the blood that comes out when you cut yourself, but it could also look dark red or brown. You can't see the egg or the womb-lining or anything exciting like that — it all just looks like a bunch of bog-standard blood.

• A period normally lasts anything from two days to a week.

• Some girls bleed lots and lots, others don't bleed much at all.

• Women usually have their periods regularly, about once a month, but when you first start getting them, the chances are that they'll be very irregular and you probably won't have the foggiest idea when your next one is due.

• When you've got your period, you'll need to use something to catch the flow of blood. You can choose between *sanitary towels* and *tampons*.

• Sanitary towels are long, flat, soft pads with a sticky strip underneath to fix them inside your pants. They catch and absorb your blood. You can buy towels in supermarkets, general stores and chemists, and there's often such a huge choice of brands, absorbencies, thicknesses and shapes that it can seem quite confusing. Most people try a few types until they find a favourite. The only guideline to follow is that if you bleed lots and lots, it's best to pick a towel that is extra thick or extra absorbent (sometimes called "super"). Some varieties of towel are called "deodorant" and they smell nice — although many people believe that this scent can irritate the delicate skin between your legs, and prefer to avoid them. Others have "wings" — little sticky side-flaps that you stick *underneath* the gusset of your pants. These are pretty good because they stop the towel from bunching up when you move around, so there's no chance at all of blood staining your pants. Many have something called a "stay-dry" top layer, which means that once the blood is absorbed into the towel, it can't squish out again, so you won't feel damp.

The advantage of towels is that they're simple to use, risk-free, and you know for sure when they need changing. There are no real disadvantages, although some people think they feel "bulky" or worry about leaking.

• A tampon is a short, fat stick of cotton wool with a string at one end for pulling it out. It fits snugly inside your vagina and absorbs the blood before it can come out. You can buy tampons from all the same shops that sell towels, and again, there's lots of choice. The two basic types are those with an *applicator* (a plastic or cardboard tube thingy that helps you push the tampon inside you) and those without (which you just push in with your finger). It's worth trying both so that you can find out which you prefer. Tampon companies often advertise special trial offers in teenage girls' magazines, where you can write off for a free sample. Tampons also come in different thicknesses. This doesn't mean the actual size, but how much blood they can absorb. If you have very heavy periods, go for a "super" tampon, otherwise "regular" is fine. Many brands also have a type called "slender", which are slimmer, easier to put in, and especially good for younger girls.

All tampons come with very good, detailed

instructions of how to put them in, and once you've got the hang of it, it only takes a second. Never worry about "losing" a tampon inside you — it's impossible! If you have trouble getting one out (like if the string goes inside you) you can always gently reach inside your vagina with your thumb and forefinger and try to pull it out that way. If you're having no luck and panicking, your doctor can do it for you — they're used to it.

The advantage of tampons is that they're totally hidden, even if you wear tight clothes, and once they're in, you can't feel them at all. The downside is that you can give yourself an infection if your fingers aren't clean when you push one in (without an applicator) or take it out. There is also a small risk of getting a very nasty, serious thing called *Toxic Shock Syndrome*, especially if you accidentally leave a tampon in for too long (we're talking days here, not hours). The leaflets in boxes of tampons explain it all in detail, but the main thing to remember is that if you throw up or feel sick, get a high temperature, feel faint, pass out or get a body-rash while you're using tampons, you must take the tampon out and call your doctor or go to a hospital immediately. If you get any of these symptoms in between periods, you should always check for a forgotten tampon and get medical help if you find one. If left untreated, TSS can kill you.

• You should always change a tampon every few hours. If you're scatty and you think you might forget, you might be better off using towels.

• Even if you prefer tampons, it's a good idea to switch to sanitary towels at night.

• Some people don't feel any discomfort at all when they get their periods, some just feel the odd strange, pulling sensation low in their tummies, while others get terrible "period pains" — nasty low-down stomach cramps. You can also get backache, feel sick, get dizzy and even get a bit sweaty and feverish. If your period pains or other symptoms are really bad, the best thing to do is lie down with a hot water bottle on your tum or back until you feel better, although some people find that going for a walk or getting some other kind of exercise can help just as much. You can also get over-the-counter pain-killers at the chemist that are designed especially for period cramps. It's nice to know that you won't neccesarily have painful periods for the rest of your life — many women find that things get much better as they get older.

• Some people find that they get grumpy, tearful, tired or depressed, and can feel "bloated" a couple of weeks *before* their period comes. This is called *Pre-Menstrual Syndrome*, and it's vile. Sometimes just knowing *why* you're feeling so bad can help you to cope, but if you find it unbearable, it's worth chatting with your doctor, who might be able to help out. Many women swear by a natural remedy called Evening Primrose Oil, which is available in capsules from health-food shops and many big chemists.

• Period pains and PMS are no joke. If you feel like you need to stay home, or just take things a bit easier than normal, you have every right.

• As long as you feel okay, your period shouldn't interfere with your life at all — it's fine to do *everything* you'd normally do. There are lots of myths about things you should avoid during your period — such as swimming, having sex, washing your hair or having a bath. Ignore them. These myths aren't just silly, they're downright unhelpful. In fact, swimming can be great for relieving period cramps and bathing (or showering or just washing) is *essential*, otherwise all that blood is going to go stale, and you'll end up pretty stinky downstairs — not nice.

HELP!

Almost everyone finds *something* that worries them about their bodies during puberty. Here's just a handful of the most common concerns:

Boys

My willy looks normal until it gets hard. Then it has a bend in it. Is there something wrong?
No — willies come in many shapes. There are probably as many around with a bend as there are straight ones, and they all work exactly the same.

My balls appear to be different sizes, and one hangs down lower than the other. Am I normal?
Totally. No one has a perfectly matching pair of balls, and no one's balls hang exactly side-by-side.

Can you break your willy?
Not exactly, because it doesn't have a bone inside it to break (although in the USA, an erection is sometimes rather misleadingly called a *boner*). Nevertheless, it's still important to be a bit careful with your willy when it's hard, because it can get damaged — and be *very* painful — if it gets violently squished or bashed at an angle.

I'm a bit worried. If the tube inside my willy can let out both wee and spunk, how does my body know which one to let out at the right time?
It just does, so don't panic about accidentally weeing inside your partner during sex or ejaculating in a public toilet when you were just planning on having a wee! Both the wee-tube and the semen-tube have little gates at the end of them, and only one can be open at a time. Your body always makes sure it's the right one.

Being circumcised never bothered me until I told some friends who weren't. They told me that it means my willy is smaller, I can't wank, and that I won't be able to enjoy sex. Are they right?

No way. Circumcision doesn't affect the length or width of your willy — in fact, when a willy is hard, it's darn near impossible to tell the difference between one with a foreskin and one without. Moreover, you can enjoy masturbation and sex just as much as someone who isn't circumcised. There are even a few *advantages* to not having a foreskin. Firstly, you won't have the problem of bodily secretions collecting under your foreskin to create a slightly pongy white mass. The word for this gunk is *smegma*, but it's often known in slang terms as *cock-cheese*. However, this doesn't mean that circumcised boys can get away with not washing their willys — you should do that anyway! It's also been medically proven that you are less likely to get infections in your reproductive organs or bladder.

I think my willy is abnormally small. I've seen other people's, and they've all been loads bigger.
On average most willies are about the same size. For the record, that's two or three inches when they're soft, and about six when they're stiff. Sure, some people are going to have bigger ones, and - yes - some are going to have smaller ones, but it's unlikely that yours is as preposterously tiny as you think. Bear in mind that when you see other people's willies you're seeing them from a different angle. You're looking *across* at theirs, and *down* at your own, which is going to make yours seem a bit smaller, and everyone else's a bit larger — it's an optical illusion. Remember too that your tackle compresses and tucks itself closer to your body when

you're feeling jumpy, tense or cold — so if you've been doing your comparisons in communal changing-rooms or showers, you've probably started with that disadvantage anyway! Even if your willy really is smaller, bear in mind that it could still grow some more if you haven't yet finished going through puberty. Most of all, though, remember that size really *isn't* important.

But don't girls prefer big willies to small ones?
Actually, if a girl hasn't had many sexual experiences, she's likely to find sex much more comfortable (and therefore more enjoyable) if her partner has a slightly smaller one. Generally, most girls and women would agree that willy size doesn't have a lot to do with how much they enjoy sex. There is a saying that goes: "It's not the size, it's what you do with it that counts". This is true, and it's also not just what you do with your *willy* that counts either: it's what you do with your hands, your mouth, your whole body and just the way you behave. If you're thoughtful, affectionate and sexy in bed, it really doesn't matter if you've got a dick like a crayon or a giant salami. It's also important to remember that girls get a great deal of their nicest sexual feelings not in their vaginas (where your willy goes) but in their clitorises — which you touch with your hands, mouth or groin — not your willy.

I saw a thing on TV about surgery that can make your willy bigger. I've also heard about creams and machines

you can buy that do the same thing. Does any of this stuff really work?
There is no cream or contraption that can make your willy bigger, although that doesn't stop some dodgy manufacturers from making products that claim to. At best, the rubbish they sell is just a waste of time and money. At worst, you could end up damaging your equipment — so steer clear. Surgery for penis enlargement does indeed exist, although at the moment it's only done in America. It's an expensive procedure which involves snipping a tendon at the base of your willy, and although it leaves you slightly bigger, many people who have had it have complained that their sex lives have got *worse*, because their willy goes flopping all over the place, and they can't control it. You've also got to remember that having a general anaesthetic can be risky, and that *any* surgery is painful, can leave you scarred, and carries big risks of infection and human error. That's why it's *never* worth having surgery you don't really need. Learn to love your willy and respect yourself, and don't let the money-grabbing people who invent these fads take advantage of your insecurities.

I get erections a lot for no particular reason, when I'm least expecting it. It's a nightmare at school, because people make fun of me. Help!
If it's any comfort, rest assured that you're perfectly normal, and it won't go on forever. Some boys find that if they can get a chance to masturbate (and come), before school it keeps their willy nice and quiet for the

rest of the day! Otherwise, it's just a question of minimising the embarrassment. As soon as you realise you've got a stiffy, find an excuse to sit down (with your hands over your lap!) until it goes. If you can't sit down, put your hands in your pockets and stretch the fabric right out. You could also try thinking about something boring and totally unsexy (like homework, chores, the bus timetable, smelly socks) — it might help speed the unwanted erection on its way.

It's a shame your classmates are so insensitive and stupid. Still, when everyone else hits puberty, it's bound to happen more often, and to other people, and the (rather cheap and childish) joke will wear thin eventually. Whatever, neither the teasing nor the erections will go on forever — so hang on in there!

I reckon I've been through just about every change in puberty but I've never had a wet dream. Does this mean my willy's not working properly?
Your willy is fine — not everyone has wet dreams. It could be that you *are* having wet dreams, though, and just haven't noticed, perhaps because you're having them early and the damp patch has dried before you wake up.

Oh my god I think I'm growing bosoms! Am I turning into a girl?
No. You're just experiencing a common, harmless but rather annoying condition which happens to a lot of

boys in puberty. What happens is that little pads of extra fat grow behind one or both nipples, stay a while, then disappear. There's nothing wrong with you, you're no less "manly" than the next bloke, and your little bosom things will go away eventually, so it's really no big deal in the great scheme of things, even though it's probably very embarrassing and horrible right now. Sadly, there's not much you can do apart from getting a nice selection of baggy tops and waiting, although you may want to visit the doctor, too, just to put your mind at rest.

My dad hasn't got any hair on his chest, and I'm not showing any signs of getting any either. Meanwhile, my mate has grown lots, and I feel a bit wimpy next to him, and worry that girls won't like me once I get my top off.
If you suspect that your dad's lack of hair has been passed down to you, you're probably right. Having a smooth chest certainly doesn't make you any "wimpier" than anyone else, and as far as which looks better — it's just a matter of taste. Remember that if a girl likes you enough to get into a "top-off" situation, then she's not going to be put off by what's under your togs, even if she prefers hairy chests to smooth ones.

Looking at the posters that my sisters pin up on their walls, I've noticed that most famous men and male models have smooth chests. It looks like I'm going to be pretty hairy, and I'm a bit worried that it'll put girls off.

Yes, lots of famous men have smooth chests, but lots don't. Sometimes it can be hard to tell exactly what people have, because lots of male models, pop stars and other men who get photographed without their tops on, actually shave their chests to get the smooth look. This is because it happens to be in fashion right now, but in a few years time they'll probably all be frantically sticking on chest-wigs. The bottom line is that fashions really aren't worth worrying about. Although some girls might prefer smooth to hairy, or hairy to smooth, most really don't give a monkey's about what's on your chest — if they fancy you, they're going to fancy you regardless.

I'm growing quite a lot of facial hair, and I want to start shaving. What do I need?

Firstly, a razor of some sort — either a disposable safety razor or one you can change the blades on, (which you use to shave when your face is wet), or an electric shaver (which you use dry). If you want to wet-shave, you could get some shaving foam, too. You can use lather from a bar of soap instead, but some blokes find it makes their skin go a bit dry and flaky. What you really *don't* need is aftershave — it serves no real purpose, it stings, and it can irritate and dry your skin. If your skin gets blotchy or itchy after shaving, you might want to use some sort of moisturiser or soothing shaving balm afterwards, instead.

GIRLS

Is there any way to tell when you're going to start your periods?
Not really, although most girls start at around the same age as their mothers did, or slightly earlier. You could also keep a look out for discharge (a little white stain in your pants). It's usually a sign that all your internal bits are kicking into gear, so if you have it regularly, the chances are that your periods will start within the next year or so.

I have discharge, but it's not white, and it smells funny. Is this normal?
Normal discharge can be off-white, but it shouldn't smell of anything in particular when it comes out (although once it dries on your knickers it sure doesn't smell of roses!). If you are a little itchy downstairs as well, you might have a vaginal infection. This isn't anything terrible, but a trip to the doctor could be in order to help clear it up. There's no need to be embarrassed about vaginal infections — everyone gets one at some point, and you don't necessarily get them from having sex (although smelly, itchy discharge can be a sign of some sexually-transmitted diseases too — see Chapter Eight for more details).

Would I be right in thinking that if I haven't started my periods, I'm not releasing eggs yet, so I can't get

pregnant if I have sex?
No, no, no! You *can* get pregnant without ever having had a period. Think about it: you release your first ripe egg a couple of weeks *before* your first period, and if you have sex around that time, you could easily get pregnant. You won't have the foggiest idea about when you're going to release your first egg, so you'll need to take as much care as someone who is already having periods.

Can girls have wet dreams?
Sex researchers reckon that you can indeed have an orgasm while you're asleep and dreaming. Chances are, though, that you wouldn't know it, as girls don't leave the obvious physical evidence that boys do — i.e. no wet patch on the bed.

I think there's something wrong with me because my nipples go inwards instead of sticking out...
You have what's called inverted nipples, and there's nothing wrong with you at all — lots of people have them. They may stay inverted all your life, or change when you get older. Either way, they're not a problem and they won't make any difference to your enjoyment of sex or your ability to breastfeed a baby.

I feel like a freak because one of my boobs is bigger than the other...

Everybody has one bigger than other, and the chances are that you're the only person that has noticed yours because you've spent ages studying them! If the size-difference is really enormous, rest assured that they'll probably even up a bit more before they finish growing.

How do I know when I need a bra?
If your boobs feel uncomfortable when you run or play sports, you could definitely do with a bra. Otherwise, it's entirely up to you whether you want to wear one or not: if you just fancy wearing one, treat yourself; if you hate the idea, don't bother. It's true that if you wear a bra every day, as soon as your bosoms have grown (regardless of their size) they won't get droopy so quickly as you get older. However, everyone's bosoms drop eventually — they would even if you wore a bra 24 hours a day from the minute you were born — so is it really worth it? Besides, there's nothing wrong with droopy boobs — many women actually find that they *prefer* the shape of theirs when they get a bit lower, rounder, fuller and softer.

I'm sixteen and my bosoms haven't changed size for two years. Is that it, then?
Not necessarily. Bosoms are one part of you (or two parts!) that change shape throughout your life. You could get another growth spurt later on in your teens, or even in your early 20s. The size and shape of your bosoms can also be affected by putting on or losing

weight, going on the pill, getting pregnant, breast-feeding or just getting older.

My boobs are small. I wish they were bigger...
Why? All bosoms feel equally nice when they're touched, and size makes no difference to breastfeeding. Little bosoms are just as feminine, attractive and sexy as big ones. Both have been in and out of fashion so many times that it's not worth even thinking about. If you're worried about boys' attitudes, sure — some prefer big ones, but an equal amount prefer small ones. Most just like bosoms, full stop, and are more interested in what they're attached to, anyway. Any intelligent, nice bloke isn't going to be swayed one way or another by the contents of your bra. Stop beating yourself up and learn to love yourself the way you are.

A friend told me that going on the pill can make your boobs grow. Is it true?
Some girls find that it makes their bosoms grow, due to the big dose of hormones, but it's not all that common. Most girls experience no change in bosom size at all, and others find that it just makes them put on a load of weight all over. It's definitely not worth going on the pill just because you want bigger boobs. For more about the pill — and its side-effects — check out Chapter Five.

What about that operation you can have to make your boobs bigger?

Getting breast implants is not something you should rush into. We're talking about a serious surgical procedure under general anaesthetic (i.e. you get put to sleep). Your bosoms are cut open, the nipples removed, and plastic bags containing either saline (sterile salt-water) or, more usually, silicone (a kind of squishy plastic) are put in before you get sewn back up again. Afterwards, you're bandaged up and it can take weeks or months for all your bruises and pain to go away. Depending on how good the surgeon was, you could be left with permanent scars. All sorts of things can go wrong — your stitches can get infected, your chest-muscles can get hard and lumpy around the bags, the bags can escape and end up somewhere else on your body (a very funny idea, unless it happens to you) and they can leak or burst inside you, which can be extremely dangerous. The surgery is expensive (implants aren't available on the NHS unless you've lost a breast through disease, or in an accident) and even if all goes swimmingly, remember that your new, big bosoms will actually be big, fake lumps of plastic that don't look or feel 100% real.

If you are truly desperate for bigger boobs, buy a padded bra, or stuff a pair of socks or some tissues in a regular bra — it's cheap, effective, risk-free, and easily reversed if you feel like going back to your original size.

My boobs are too big! I wish they were smaller...

As with people who feel that their bosoms are too small, the best thing you can do is try to learn to love yourself the way you are, and try not worry about it too much. Buy a good, supporting bra for comfort and try to avoid the temptation to hunch over or slouch — it won't hide your bosoms, and could cause you horrible problems with your back. Hopefully when you get a bit older you might have a change of attitude anyway, and feel less embarrassed and more proud of your bosoms.

What about breast-reduction surgery?
Yes, you can have an operation to make your bosoms smaller. Like any operation, there are a few risks involved, but it's generally simpler and safer than having your bosoms made bigger. It's still expensive, but if the NHS reckons that your case is worthy, it *is* possible to get it done for free. To qualify, you'd need to have *very* large boobs and be able to prove that they were horribly uncomfortable, stopped you from enjoying everyday activities, made you feel terribly depressed, and perhaps gave you problems with bad-posture and back pains. You would need to have a doctor's report, so the first step would be to have a chat with your GP.

I'm not keen on all this new body hair. What's the best way of dealing with it?
You don't *have* to get rid of body hair — millions of women choose not to. If you want to, though, there are lots of different ways. Like:

• Shaving — easy and cheap (all you need is a disposable razor and some soap lather). Good for leg and armpit hairs, and okay for what's rather coyly known as your "bikini-line" (i.e. the pubic hair that shows when you wear knickers or a swimsuit). The hair grows back in a few days, and feels a bit bristlier than before.

• Depilatory lotion — gunk that dissolves leg and armpit hair. (You can also get a gentler kind for your bikini-line.) It's easy to use, and hairs grow back more slowly and less bristly than if you'd shaved.

• Waxing — putting a special wax on your legs, armpits or bikini-line, then ripping it off — with all your hairs in it. Ouch! You can buy a waxing kit (which can be tricky to get the hang of), or have it done by a beautician (which can be costly). Hair grows back slowly, though, (it takes a couple of weeks) and feels soft, because it's brand new hair.

• Electric depilators — little electric gadgets that you run over your legs, they catch the hairs and pull them out from the root. This has all the benefits of waxing, only it's easier, and cheaper in the long run (once you've bought the gadget, that's it for life).

I've grown some hairs on my face, and I'm not happy. What can I do?
You can pluck them out with tweezers, use facial

depilatory creams or waxing kits or, if you're fair skinned, lighten the hairs with a special facial bleach to make them less noticeable. There's also electrolysis — a simple procedure done by a qualified beautician, where the hairs get zapped at the root by a little electric beam and hopefully stay away for good. However, you need a course of treatments, and it's not cheap — think carefully.

Warning: if you have a hair growing from a mole, snip it off with scissors. Never pluck or wax it — moles are funny things that are best left alone.

What about hair around the nipples or tummy?
Follow all the same rules as for facial hair.

Can I use deodorant between my legs?
Nooo! Don't even try it! You're talking about a *really* sensitive area that could easily get irritated, and besides, you don't *need* deodorant down there. Just a regular wash every day will keep everything smelling nice.

WHEN YOU'RE REALLY WORRIED...

As you can see, most of the stuff that worries us is perfectly normal and not really worth fretting about. However, if something's bugging you a lot, and you just can't get it out of your mind, or you really feel that something might be wrong with you, it's always worth a visit to your doctor. It's a sad fact that many people avoid visiting their GP, for all sorts of reasons. You might be embarrassed about your problem, and wonder how the doctor will react. You might feel worried that if there *is* something wrong, you might not really want to know about it, or that if there isn't, the doctor might be cross with you for wasting his or her time. You should never let these — or any other — fears put you off visiting the doctor. If a problem is worrying you, it's always worth checking out, just to put your mind at rest, and that's what doctors are there for. Gather up your courage, and just remember:

• Doctors have seen everything before, and they never find anything surprising, disgusting or funny — they're very matter-of-fact.

• A doctor will never laugh at you, tell you you're being silly, deliberately embarrass you or tell you off (for time-wasting or anything else).

• If it turns out that you *do* have a problem, it's always better to know about it. Almost every problem can be sorted out, and you'll feel so much better knowing that it's being dealt with and that you don't have to worry any more.

• If it turns out that you *don't* have a problem, you'll be able to forget all about it and get on with your life without wasting all that energy on worrying.

• Doctors get paid for seeing patients — that's their job. Every day, they'll be visted by some people with serious problems, some people with simple problems, and some who turn out to have no problem at all. A doctor will be used to seeing all of them.

Chapter Two

The New You

It's not just your body that changes during puberty. The way you feel changes too, and that can be even more confusing. Suddenly you're discovering feelings you've never had before, thinking new thoughts, worrying about new problems. Sometimes it can feel like you're changing so much, and so quickly, that you hardly know yourself any more.

Probably long before you even consider having sex, you'll find yourself thinking and wondering about it, asking yourself more and more questions. You'll discover all sorts of things about what kinds of people you fancy and what excites you, and perhaps you'll get to know your own body better sexually, by *masturbating* — touching your private parts because it feels nice.

What's really going on is that you're turning into the person you're going to be for the rest of your life — the adult-you, the new you. Getting to know the new you is just like getting to know someone else — interesting, complicated and sometimes surprising. It's a huge task that's partly a wonderful, thrilling adventure and partly a huge, confusing pain in the bum. But it's one of the most important things you'll ever do, because the more you understand and feel comfortable with yourself, the easier it'll be to help other people to get to know you, and know what you want out of a relationship. And that's the key to having a fantastic, happy and secure love-life in the future.

YOUR FEELINGS

Just as everyone frets over whether their bodies are "normal", we all wonder if what's going on in our heads is what's supposed to be going on. Here are some very common worries...

I think about sex all the time. Am I normal?
You bet! You see, the hormones that cause all the physical changes in your body during puberty don't just make you sprout hairs and suchlike. They also get working on your brain, and bingo — you've got urges like you've never felt before. Quite apart from this, sex is jolly interesting, and thinking about it can be a very nice, exciting thing to do with your spare time! Even if you can believe that you're perfectly healthy and normal, thinking about sex all the time can still make you feel uneasy, because you can feel that you're losing control of your brain. It happens like this: at first you find you think about sex a bit, and it's fine. Then it starts popping into your head of its own accord. You

don't mind that either, and nor do you care much when it starts distracting you in dull moments — after all, it's far more fascinating and fun to think about sex than, say, algebra. But time goes on and you suddenly realise you're even thinking about sex at times when you would have been thinking about stuff you *liked* — such as who's going to win Saturday's football match, what happened on EastEnders last night, whether you can beat your brother's hi-score on Sonic II. It can feel like sex is invading your life, changing the way you are — or thought your were — as a person, and it's a scary feeling. Just as you can't stop the changes taking place in your body, you can't stop what's happening in your head. It's still your brain, but right now it's like a computer trying to process all sorts of complicated new software that's been dumped onto its hard-drive in the middle of a huge power-surge. It's going to take a little bit of time before everything gets sorted and you can go back to using it for whatever you want, but it *will* happen. By all means, look around for other new interests you can throw yourself into for distraction. Otherwise, just try to relax and carry on with your life.

I'm not interested in sex at all. Is there something wrong with me?

Not a sausage. There are a hundred degrees of "normal", and whilst it's perfectly healthy to have your brain teeming with sexy thoughts, it's equally healthy — and equally common — not to have the slightest tad of interest whatsoever. If sex is the furthest thing from your mind, it could be because your hormones haven't kicked in yet, or it could be that they have, but you're not affected as strongly as the next person. Equally, it could be that you've got a busy life with so many other interests that you just haven't got the time and energy to spare for thinking about sex. In any case, the chances are that a day will come when sex plays a bigger part in your thoughts and your life, one way or another.

Certainly there are some people who never get very interested in sex, and make a conscious choice that sex is not going to be a part of their life. These people are usually happy and confident about their decision. If the thought that you might never want sex makes you panic or feel sad, then it's very unlikely that you'll turn out that way. The mere fact that you're worrying shows that sex *is* important to you, and it's likely that your natural urges will hit you in the future.

I often imagine having sex with people I know, or famous people. I really enjoy it. Is it okay?
It's called fantasising. It's more than okay, and nearly everybody does it at some time in their life. It's just like daydreaming, only its main purpose is to make you feel excited in a sexual way.

A fantasy can be about anyone and anything. It can be a quick thought that pops into your head for a moment, or a long, detailed story that goes on for ages in your head. In other words, thinking for a second what it might be like to snog your teacher is a fantasy, and so is spending twenty minutes imagining passionate sex with all the members of your favourite pop group in a big bath full of melted chocolate.

Some people fantasise just for fun, others like to do it while they masturbate, and find that it makes them feel even more excited than if they were just touching themselves. In fact, many people find that what goes on in their heads can excite them just as much as what's going on down below. Many, many people also fantasise while they're having sex (see Chapter Six).

Fantasising is a fantastically healthy way to discover more about your own sexual feelings, so you should never feel guilty about doing it.

If you fantasise about something, does it mean that you really want it to happen?

No way. Once people get into fantasising, they often find their thoughts getting wilder and wilder and involving people or activities that they definitely wouldn't want to get involved with in real life. It's a very common, very healthy thing — it means you're exploring the boundaries of your imagination and finding out what excites you.

People are often surprised by what excites them in a fantasy, and can even find themselves getting turned on by an idea that would normally horrify them. When this happens, you can feel pretty disgusted at yourself and wonder how you could even have *thought* of such a thing, let alone got excited. If you find it totally impossible to shake off your guilty feelings about a particular fantasy, it's obviously better to give it a rest than be miserable. Generally, though, you should never beat yourself up about what goes on in your head. Remember that you're healthy and normal, and that a fantasy never hurt anyone.

So any fantasy is fine? Even a really weird one?
Sure. And the chances are that your "weird" fantasy has already been thought of by a trillion other people. Here are just a few popular fantasies: having sex with parents, with brothers or sisters, with close friends, with strangers, with people you don't even like; having sex with lots of people at the same time; having sex with an animal, or being licked by one; watching other people have sex; having others watch you while you have sex, do a striptease or play with yourself; being paid to have sex; visiting a prostitute; being tied-up or forced to have sex or doing it to someone else.

The only time you should worry about your fantasies is if they are very violent, and get more violent. If you get turned on thinking about injuring or killing animals or people, you might have a problem, and you need to talk to a professional counsellor or therapist as soon as possible.

I'm having a lot of rude dreams. What's up?
You might have guessed it – rude dreams are yet another trick that your hormones are playing on your brain. Not to mention the fact that if sex is in your thoughts more often these days, then it's bound to be in

your dreams too. Dreams are often harder to cope with than fantasies because you can't control what you dream about. You can find that you're having rude dreams about all sorts of people and situations that you wouldn't touch with a barge pole but, as with fantasies, it doesn't mean that deep down you want these things to happen — it's just your imagination doing a bit of exploring all by itself! It can be weird, but try not to let it bug you too much. Sometimes a rude dream can stay in your head all day, and facing someone you've dreamt about can be embarrassing. Just remember, though, that no one can tell you've had a rude dream, so there's nothing to worry about!

I've fancied people in the past but now there's one person I can't stop thinking about and I feel like I'm going crazy. What's going on? Is this love?
Sort of. It's actually what's called a *crush* or *infatuation*, and it's another mental side-effect of all this growing up your body is doing. It's like a little test-run for all the complicated emotions you're about to start feeling. What's the difference between love and a crush? In very simple terms, love is what happens when you get to know someone really well and are having a relationship with them. A crush is a feeling you get about someone you're not having a relationship with — like a teacher, a famous person, a friend or someone you see regularly but don't know that well. You might fantasise about going out with that person, kissing them, having sex with them or even living with them or marrying them!

You'd think that a crush wouldn't feel as intense as love, but actually it can be equally as exciting, confusing and exhausting — if not more so, because it's all going on in your head, instead of in real life, and you're not getting any feed-back.

Crushes can be wonderful — your heart leaps when you see the object of your desire, just talking about them or thinking about them makes you happy, you feel warm and bursting with passion.

Crushes can also be hideous — you feel desperate to be with that person, miserable, lonely and frustrated because you're not or can't be, and despairing because you can't imagine you'll ever feel the same way about anyone else. Everyone who has ever had a crush experiences both the good *and* the bad side, and, unfortunately, there's very little you could do to "get rid of" a crush. Luckily, though, crushes don't last forever. You *will* find someone else you feel strongly about, and with any luck they'll feel the same way about you and it'll be a million times nicer — honest!

STRAIGHT, GAY OR BISEXUAL?

Research shows that about 90-98% of the population fancy people of the opposite sex. They're called *heterosexual* or *hetero*, or *straight*. The other 2-10% are sexually attracted to people of their own sex. They're called *homosexual*, or *gay*, and if they're female, they can also be called *lesbian*. There are also plenty of slang words like *homo, bent, bender, poof, fag, woofter, lezzie, dyke* or *queer*, and other ruder, more jokey names, too — usually describing sexual things that gay people might get up to. All these are pretty insulting, and anyone with half a brain wouldn't use them, although dyke and queer are becoming more acceptable these days, as they're often used by gay people themselves.

Many people are attracted to *both* sexes. The word for this is *bi-sexual* (pronounced "bye"-sexual), or *bi* for short.

Being gay or bi shouldn't make your life any more complicated than anyone else's, but unfortunately it can and often does, largely because of other people's bad attitudes and hang-ups. Wondering if you might be gay shouldn't be a traumatic thing, but this sad fact means that it usually is. Still, just trying to make sense of your own feelings can be puzzling enough...

I've only ever had serious crushes on people who are the same sex as me. Does this mean I'm gay?

The way you feel now is not *necessarily* the way you'll feel for the rest of your life. Many girls and boys find that they have crushes on people of *both* sexes as they grow up, then end up being straight. Even people who *only* fancy people of the same sex and even have sexual experiences with them while they're young, sometimes wind up being straight later. Having said this, it used to be very fashionable for teachers and parents to write off same-sex crushes and relationships as "just a phase you're going through". This is unfair and a bit dodgy. A lot of people discover very young that they are gay, never doubt it and never change, so to risk writing off *their* feelings as "just a phase" is rather snotty and dismissive. It's also worth remembering that a lot of gay adults went through their teens having only heterosexual feelings, and discovered their true feelings later, so being straight when you're young could fairly be described as "just a phase" too!

For now, do yourself a favour and try to resist the temptation to "label" yourself as any one thing or another. Remember that when you're attracted to someone, it's hopefully not just about what's between their legs. Perhaps you *won't* ever find you fancy anyone of the opposite sex, and will decide one day that you are definitely gay, but for now you certainly don't have to pin yourself down and put yourself in a pigeon-hole if you don't want to.

The world would surely be a much easier place to live in if we stopped making a big deal about our differences, and looked at our similarities instead. After all, we're all just *people* who get attracted to other *people*, and what sex anyone is should be no more important than what colour hair they have.

I've got a crush on my teacher, who is the same sex as me. Apart from that, I only fancy people of the opposite sex. Does this mean I'm bi-sexual?

Maybe, but again, don't worry too much about it — you've got plenty of time to find out. Many psychologists believe that *everyone* is bi-sexual, whether or not we choose to do anything about it. A huge amount of straight adults will have had had a crush on someone of the same gender.

Crushes aren't always sexual, anyway. You can feel very passionate about someone because you admire them, think they are attractive and clever, and wish you could be just like them. You usually get this kind of crush on a teacher, prefect or other older person, and it doesn't necessarily mean that you want to have sex with them.

I'm pretty sure I'm gay. Should I tell my friends?
Telling people that you're gay is sometimes called *coming out*, and there's no "should" about it. If you want to share your feelings with them, then do. If you don't, then you've got every right not to. It's a hard decision to make, because you don't know how they're going to react. It's a sad fact that people are often very uptight and uneasy about things they can't understand, and that can make them act like class-A tossers. If you can make your friends understand you, you've won half the battle. You might need to remind them that you're still exactly the same person, and even though you may be different to them in one way, life is not all about sex, and you still have all the same things in common as you had before.

Friends of the same sex may also wonder if you fancy *them* and feel funny. Yes, it's stupid, and it's their problem, but it's still a good idea to make it clear that you don't.

If your friends tease or reject you, they're not worth hanging on to anyway. Having no friends at all isn't a nice thought, but it really is far better than having ignorant, useless, uncaring ones.

I think I might be gay, but I'm very confused. I'd love to have someone to talk to about my feelings, but I don't know who would understand.
When you're trying to get to grips with anything at all, the best person to talk to is someone who has been in the same situation themselves. If you don't know anyone who is openly gay, don't worry — there are some excellent gay help-lines you can phone (see the addresses section at the end of this book). These lines are staffed by gay people who are also trained counsellors, and will be understanding, helpful and very easy to talk to.

How can you tell if someone is gay?
You can't. There are plenty of myths about what gay people look like or how they behave — i.e. gay men are feminine, dress oddly, talk in "camp" voices like Julian Clary, and walk around wiggling their bums with one hand flopping in front of them; lesbians are "butch" and wear men's clothes, huge boots, have very short haircuts and talk in a fierce growly voice. These are just silly stereotypes, and very few gay people actually fit them. Most look, talk and dress exactly the same as the next person — because apart from who they choose to

go to bed with (which is really nobody else's business), they *are* the same.

MASTURBATING

You might well have heard about masturbating before. Some people call it *playing with yourself, fiddling with yourself, bringing yourself off* or *wanking.* Boys sometimes call it *jerking off, tossing*, or *having one off the wrist* and very old-fashioned adults sometimes refer to it as *self-abuse*, which is a stupid term, because there's nothing harmful or bad about it.

Masturbating basically means touching or rubbing your private parts to give yourself pleasure, and often — but not always — an orgasm.

These are some of the many things that people want to know:

What's an orgasm?

An orgasm, also known as *coming* or *climaxing*, is what happens when you've reached the highest point of sexual excitement. It sounds like a really big deal — and it can feel like one too — but it's surprisingly easy to make it happen. Here's how it goes: you'll find that when you touch your penis or clitoris, in certain ways, it feels nice. If you carry on doing whatever it was that felt nice, you'll find it starts feeling better and better, and that's when you start to get a feeling that *something* is going to happen. It's a little bit like when you know for sure that you're going to sneeze. When you've become as physically excited as you can possibly get, that's when it happens — a really big, but quite quick, ultra-lovely feeling that happens in your genitals, but sends waves through your whole body. After you've had an orgasm, you feel a huge sense of release that is very satisfying — again, a bit like sneezing, only a million times more enjoyable. It's quite hard to imagine what having an orgasm is like until you've actually had one, but once you have, you suddenly understand your body a lot better and will always find it quite easy in the future to recognise when you're about to come.

Is masturbating normal?

Utterly, utterly normal. Very nearly as normal as eating, sleeping and using the loo. Almost everybody does it at some time or another, and many people of all ages do it regularly and often. You probably first discovered that it felt nice to touch your bits, or rub them up against things when you were a very little kid, but then you got interested in other things, and forgot all about it for a while. Most people re-discover the joys of playing with themselves around the time when they hit puberty, and spend the next few years doing it a great deal. Once you hit adulthood, you'll probably do it a bit less often, but most people carry on doing it for the rest of their lives.

Is it harmful?
Far from it. It's actually very useful, because it teaches you to understand how your body works, and what feels nice for you, sexually. It's also very good for you, psychologically, to do something that's so nice for yourself. Just as having sex can be a way of showing how much you love someone else, masturbation is a way of showing how much you love yourself — and people who love themselves are the happiest, healthiest people of all. Psychology boffins say that before you can have a good, healthy adult relationship with anyone else, you have to care about yourself — and what better way of proving it than to make yourself feel nice by masturbating.

So it's not harmful at all? But I heard...
Yeah, yeah, there are a million rumours about what terrible things masturbation can do to you. Perhaps you've been told that it makes you go blind, or become short-sighted. Or that it stops you from ever being able to make babies, rots your brain cells, sends you insane, damages your genitals, makes them shrink, ruins your chances of having a normal sex-life or gives you some other nasty medical ailment or disease. Boys are also sometimes told that it "uses up" all their sperm. This is all total and utter crap. There has never been any medical evidence linking masturbation with infertility, mental health or any other illness or problem, and as the average sexually mature male produces many millions of new sperms every day, it would be utterly

impossible to run out. There is not an ounce of truth in these, or any other rumours about masturbation being bad for you.

How did the rumours start, then?

They were cooked up by adults who disapproved of masturbation for any number of reasons, as a way of putting young people (and other adults who didn't agree with them) off masturbating. Some people disapproved because they felt that sex was "dirty" and that it was "wrong" to feel sexual pleasure. Others had strong religious beliefs that sex and the sexual organs only existed in order for married people to make babies, and that using the genitals for any kind of sexual pleasure — especially outside of marriage — was "sinful". There are still people about who think the same way. Of course, everyone is entitled to their own beliefs, but people also have a right to know the truth. Facts are facts, and the plain truth is that masturbation is not harmful.

So how do you do it?

There's no particular way to masturbate — everyone does it a little bit differently. Nevertheless, here are the basics:

• Boys usually do it by gripping their penis in one hand and sliding their hand up and down in a jerky motion that gets gradually faster. Boys who have a foreskin often slide it up and down over the head of their penis.

This is the basic method, but not everyone does it this way. Some boys prefer to just touch and stroke the sensitive tip of their penis. Others like to lie on their front and rub their whole body up and down against whatever they're lying on. When boys reach a peak of excitement, they have an orgasm and ejaculate — semen comes out of their willy. After a boy comes his willy will go limp and soft.

•Girls masturbate in many different ways too. Many find that their favourite is to gently but firmly rub their clitoris at a steady, rhythmic pace, gradually getting faster. Others rub the whole vaginal area, or move one or two fingers around inside their fanny. Still others put a pillow between their legs and rub up and down against it, and some girls find that they can masturbate just by crossing their legs and squeezing them together in a regular rhythm, or by clenching and unclenching their vaginal muscles (the same ones you can use to stop your wee coming out mid-stream). Like boys, girls have orgasms once they reach their peak of sexual excitement. When they come, girls feel an explosive, pleasant feeling between their legs, and might notice that the muscles down there go into a little, twitchy spasm for a moment. Afterwards, there's a lovely feeling of release and relaxation, and the clitoris usually feels a little bit tingly and sensitive.

I think the way I masturbate might be a bit strange...
Unlikely. So far we've only checked out the most basic ways of masturbating. There are a million and one more. Whatever it is you like to do, the chances are that

it's harmless, normal, and is done by a squillion other people, too! Here are just a tiny handful of the things that people do.

- Touch, rub or squeeze their nipples

- Stroke, touch or squeeze their balls

- Use soapy water, oil, cream or some other slippery liquid on their hands or genitals to make their movements smoother.

- Put an object into their fanny.

- Put their fingers or an object into their bums (girls *and* boys)

- Rub their willies in and out of toilet roll tubes, soft fruit and many other inventive items!

- Spray their clitorises with a strong jet of water, using a shower attachment or tap.

- Rub themselves against furniture, cushions, soft toys and other things.

- Sit on or press themselves up against something that vibrates (like a washing machine, dryer or other piece of machinery).

And all those things are okay?
Yeah, they're normal, and they're generally safe as long as you follow these simple rules:

• Don't let any coloured or perfumed liquid go on your privates in case it irritates them or causes a rash — choose something gentle and pure, like spit, baby oil, butter, cooking oil, a gentle soap, Vaseline or KY Jelly (from chemists).

• If you're going to put your fingers into your vagina or bottom, make sure they're clean.

• If you're going to put something other than fingers inside yourself, make sure it's clean, has no sharp edges and won't break. Never use anything made of glass or china. Go for something organic, like a vegetable (cucumbers and carrots are popular!), or something smooth and plastic (if it's a container with something in it, make sure it's done up tightly!).

• If you lose your grip on something you've put inside your vagina, don't panic. You can't lose anything up there, because it's only a few inches long and has a wall of flesh at the top. Relax, then gently slide your forefinger and thumb into your fanny (a little spit or other lubrication makes the job easier), "bear down" like you were trying to poo, and try to grasp the object. If you don't get it, keep trying — you'll get it eventually. Failing that, a doctor won't mind fishing it out for you, and won't be embarrassed about it (although you probably will be!). If it's any comfort, doctors and hospitals get regular visits from people claiming that they just happened to be sitting naked on a chair when they mysteriously fell off onto this battery/candle/ carrot!

• If you're going to put something in your bottom, the same safety rules apply, plus you should be *ultra*-careful never to use something small enough to get lost or stuck up there. Unlike a fanny, your bottom is an open passage that just keeps on going (it's basically a continuation of your lower intestine). If you lose your grip on something, it could get horribly lost. This would be quite dangerous, and you'd definitely need to visit the doctor or the casualty department at a hospital.

• If you use a shower or tap, be very careful not to let it squirt water directly *into* your vagina, as a strong jet being forced up inside you is bad news.

• If you enjoy sticking your willy into things, please choose your object with safety in mind. Cardboard tubes and fruit are safe, as is any other unbreakable item that is smooth and has a hole at both ends. Things made of glass or china aren't safe. Neither are jars, wide-necked bottles and other things with a sealed bottom, because your thrusting could create a vacuum and you could end up getting your willy completely stuck.

• You may have heard jokes or even serious

recommendations about sticking your willy into the end of the Hoover nozzle and turning it on so that it "sucks" you. Don't try it — it's dangerous.

• If you press up against electrical goods, please be sensible. Most large household appliances are perfectly okay, but industrial machinery is a total no-no — many a factory worker has met with a gruesome and tragic accident in the pursuit of fun!

Is it possible to suck your own willy?
Many boys give it a try for interests sake, but unless you have a combination of a very supple spine, a very long willy and a conveniently shaped body, it's completely impossible and you're likely to end up with little more than a horribly strained back!

If putting something inside your vagina feels nice, does that means that girls can get sexually excited when they use a tampon?
Many boys — and some girls — wonder about this. The answer is a resounding no, as anyone who has ever used a tampon can confirm. Sure, some objects feel nice going inside you, but a tampon is not one of them, because it's dry, soft and bendy. Useful, yes, exciting,no.

I masturbate a lot. Am I weird?
Not at all. Many teenagers masturbate one heck of a lot, and that's fine. If you're really worried, rest assured

that it's unlikely that you'll wank this much for the rest of your life. Once you get into a relationship, have less time on your hands or just get a bit older, you're bound to do it less. Even if you carried on this way forever, though, it wouldn't be doing you any harm, so don't panic.

I'm not really into masturbating at all. Is there something wrong with me?
Nothing. Lots of people aren't into it, and that's just as normal as being very, very keen! Although we've gone into all the reasons why masturbation is good and lovely and healthy, you're not really depriving yourself of anything if you don't do it. Having said that, a lack of interest in masturbating can be a clue to some deeper problem going on in your head, and if that's the case, it's important not to ignore it. For instance, if you feel that it's dirty or "wrong" to feel sexual pleasure, your attitudes could make you feel sad and uncomfortable when you come to have a relationship, and it could be worth trying to talk to a counsellor at some point about how you feel. Similarly, if you feel funny about sexual touching because you've been sexually abused, getting the help of a professional will give you the chance to have a perfectly happy adult life — sexually and in every other way.

Chapter Three

ATTITUDES TO SEX

Coming to terms with all these new changes and discoveries can be pretty hard work. But don't pause for breath yet! Here's something else to get a handle on: attitudes. Everyone has their own ideas and opinions when it comes to sex, and it's important to think about them because they can affect your life.

YOUR PARENTS' ATTITUDES

Even the most broadminded parents find it tricky to cope with their kids growing up to be sexual adults. On the one hand they feel uncomfortable with the idea of you having sex (and it'll be impossible to understand how they feel until you have kids of your own). On the other hand, there are all the very real worries that this precious little person that they adore (that's you) is going to be running the risk of being made unhappy by a difficult sexual relationship, or getting pregnant, or catching a sexually-transmitted disease. Parents usually start worrying about all this stuff long before they even need to. It usually only takes the discovery of a wet-dream stain on the duvet or a poster of a scantily clad pop star on the bedroom wall to convince most parents that their offspring are on the verge of shagging anything that moves.

Let's face it, parents worry. They work themselves into a frenzy worrying and it's all because they care about you. Except they then go and show it in weird ways that wind you up, like being stroppy or saying embarrassing things. No matter how strict your parents are, the key to an easy home life is to talk to them. Hopefully, by talking to them, you can convince them that you are mature enough to deal with all the problems and risks that come with sex. Most people are surprised how amenable their parents can turn out to be. Even if a parent doesn't like the idea of you having sex at all, most would rather know for sure who you were doing it with, where you were doing it and that you were using a condom, than be left in the dark to imagine the worst. If you talk to your parents from the start, you'll find that it'll be much easier to come to them for help and advice if you need it in the future.

Some parents have very strong views that young people shouldn't have sex at all, or that sex should be saved for marriage. Changing their minds is likely to be impossible. In cases like this, you're best off keeping some things secret, but that doesn't mean you should sneak around and go against what they say. If you talk to them about everything else you get up to, come home when you say you're going to, and act as mature as you possibly can, they'll hopefully give you the freedom you want anyway. You'll just have to turn elsewhere for help and advice about sex.

YOUR FRIENDS' ATTITUDES

Coming of age sexually can put a big strain on friendships. Because everyone develops at different rates, there's always bound to be someone in every group who is so full of raging hormones that they're not interested in much else *but* sex, and someone else who'd still much rather be playing football, mucking around with their computer or looking at pictures of ponies. Everyone is wondering what everyone else thinks, and what can happen pretty fast is that everyone stops being honest about how they feel because they're so worried about being seen as "normal". The saddest thing that can happen is that someone can feel so pressured to keep up with what they *think* everyone else is doing, that they go and have sex just for the sake of it, only to discover later that all their friends are actually still virgins. Gaining sexual experience is not a competition, and losing your virginity doesn't make you a member of some elite club. It's all stuff that should be done at your own pace, when you're ready, and it shouldn't matter to a friendship if one person has "gone further" than the other.

Beware of friends who set themselves up as sex experts. This is how some of the most dangerous and damaging myths and rumours about sex get spread around. Just because someone has done more than you, sexually (or claims to have), it doesn't mean that they know everything there is to know about sex. If someone tells you something, don't ever take it as gospel, especially if it sounds utterly terrifying or too good to be true (like some amazingly simple way you can avoid getting pregnant). Check it out with an adult or in a book like the one you're holding!

Other ways that your friends' attitudes can be a problem is if they are very different to yours. Everyone has their own point of view about subjects like virginity, sleeping-around, being gay, abortion, pornography and a billion others. You and your mates are bound to clash on at least a few of them, but a true friendship can survive differences in opinion, as long as you're big enough to agree to disagree!

This is a time when platonic friendships between boys and girls can get a weeny bit strained, as you start wondering if your long-time pal fancies you — or indeed if you fancy them. Even if you decide there's nothing doing, it can be surprisingly tricky and envy-making when one of you starts dating. This doesn't mean your friendship is doomed, as long as you can talk honestly and act reasonably.

THE OPPOSITE SEX

It can be very weird when you notice that the snotty-faced kid from next door who you used to make mud-pies with has suddenly turned into a rampant sexual being who blatantly stares at your bum every time you walk past. Just as you're starting to get interested in the opposite sex, they're starting to get interested in you too, and although being admired is a nice thing, it can be pretty weird, too. Of course, it *does* all depend on how people show their feelings. If someone of the opposite sex smiles at you in a friendly way or gives you a compliment, it can be a lovely, ego-boosting thing, even if you don't fancy them back. However, walking past a big group who are making rude gestures and noises or shouting out things like "Phoooar! Lovely arse!" and "I wouldn't mind giving you one!" can be one of the most completely horrible experiences in the world. In the past it's been mostly girls who have had to put up with this kind of thing, but these days you're just as likely to find a bunch of girls leering and making saucy comments. People who behave this way don't usually mean any harm — it's just a combination of wanting to have a laugh and "bond" with their mates, and not really knowing how to react when they find someone attractive. But even though all that leering and yelling isn't supposed to be threatening or embarrassing, it can certainly feel like it to the person on the receiving end. The bottom line is that everyone has the right to walk down a street or a school corridor without being made to feel uncomfortable, so if you're guilty of this kind of thing, you should really think about quitting. If you're a victim of a leery gang, the best thing you can do is hold your head up high, smile, keep walking and try to take it as a compliment — which is probably how it was intended. This is a better policy than trying to make a smart comment or getting stroppy, because the more interesting your reaction, the more it'll encourage a repeat performance in the future. If it just keeps happening, and you're really unhappy about it, you've got every right to report it. If leering and comments upset, scare or just severely irritate you, it's called *sexual harassment*, and it's taken very seriously these days. If someone really oversteps the mark (by insulting you, making a really gross and offensive comment, or by actually touching you), it's *definitely* time to summon up all your courage and self-respect and report the offender to a teacher, a superior at work or anyone else in a higher position of authority than the person or gang who is bugging you. If you can do this, you're not just protecting yourself, but anyone else who is being harassed. Uninvited touching is especially serious — it's called *sexual assault*, and it's a criminal offence, so if you wanted to tell the police, you can be sure that they'd be sympathetic.

It can be traumatic enough when people of your own age start noticing you in a sexual way, but it's even stranger and scarier when it's an adult showing a sexual interest in you. You can't help looking more grown up and sexy than you used to, and without even realising it, you could be sending out all sorts of sexual signals in the way you dress and behave. Adults can't help picking up on all those signals, but a reasonable adult will deliberately ignore any sexual stirrings they might feel for an adolescent, will work hard to hide their feelings and wouldn't dream of doing anything about it. Sadly, though, not all adults are reasonable, and some are not sensible or strong enough to stop their feelings from getting out of hand. At the very least it can be embarrassing and uncomfortable if an adult makes a leery comment or eyes you up. At worst you could find yourself the unwilling victim of something far worse, like being seriously harassed, touched up, assaulted or even raped. For more information, turn to Chapter Nine.

If you are flattered by adult attention, or attracted to the adult who is interested in you, you're looking at a potentially dangerous situation. Don't kid yourself that you could cope with any kind of sexual relationship with an adult, no matter how mature, confident and savvy you are. It's not *you* that would be the problem, it's them. Adults automatically have a kind of power over younger, more unsure people. If an adult doesn't have the good moral sense not to get involved with someone so vulnerable (and you *are* vulnerable, whatever you think), then they probably wouldn't have the decency and reason that would stop them from abusing that power and making your life a misery. Think about it.

YOUR ATTITUDES TO SEX

Even if you'd never really thought about it before, the chances are that you've already got pretty well-formed attitudes about sexuality. These attitudes have probably planted themselves in your head over the years without you even knowing it, and now that you're becoming a sexual person, it's the perfect time to drag them out, have a long hard look at them, and think them through properly. While everyone is entitled to their own opinion, there are ways of thinking that can make you go through life being thoughtless and unreasonable, hurting other people, and risking getting hurt yourself. Are you guilty of any of the deadly bad-attitude sins? Read on and find out...

Seeing Other People Only As Sex Objects

• Would you be prepared to have sex with someone who you thought was boring, dull or not very nice, just because they had a great body or attractive face?

• Would you consider it a waste of time to go out with someone who firmly refused to have sex, even if you really liked them?

• Do you think that the opposite sex is "only good for one thing"?

• Do you enjoy looking at pornography?

If you answered yes to two or more of these questions, it's quite likely that you do see people only as sex objects. While this isn't a terrible crime in itself, it's an attitude that can make you uncaring, and liable to treat others with less respect than they deserve. Even if you can't change the way you think, you can keep a check on how you behave. Using other people just for sex is a horrible thing. You not only risk hurting others, you also risk missing out on having truly fulfilling, happy relationships — because the best relationships (and the best sex) happen between two people who respect and trust each other equally. If you can't get that, get this: once people get wind of the fact that you're only after one thing and you don't mind treating your partners like dirt (and they will — people aren't stupid) you'll find that the chances of getting your leg over at all will rapidly diminish to nil. Then what?

BEING SEXIST (not seeing boys and girls as "equal", or assuming things about a person just because of their gender)

• Would you say that a girl was a "slag", "slut", "tart" or "trollop" because she sleeps around, but say he's 'sowing his wild oats' when talking about a boy?

• Do you think that most boys are just after sex and most girls are just after lovey-dovey stuff?

• If a boy turned down the chance to have sex, would you be surprised, or think he was weird?

If you answered yes to *any* of the above then you're guilty of thinking in a sexist way, at least some of the time. If you answered yes to all of them, it's pretty deeply ingrained. If you want to understand people and have a happy, unconfusing love-life, you've got to chuck out all your ideas about what girls and boys are *supposed* to be like and learn that everyone is different. There are lots of boys who'd rather have a kiss and a cuddle and wait until they get to really know and love someone before leaping into bed, and lots of girls who just adore having as much sex as possible. These people are not weirdos or slags — they're perfectly normal. Wise up.

Believing There's Such A Thing As A "Right" To Sex

• If someone gets into heavy petting, then refuses to go any further, are they a "tease"?

• If you took someone on a fantastic date and spent a lot of money on them in the process, would it be fairly reasonable to expect sex, a feel, or at least a snog?

• If your partner had waited for months on end until you felt ready to have sex, but you still weren't 100 per cent sure, should you do it anyway, as a "thank you" for their patience and understanding?

Any "yes" answers at all? You're guilty of believing that there are certain circumstances where people *should* have sex, even if they don't really want to. This is rubbish, and the kind of attitude which guarantees that someone is going to get hurt. For once and for all: *No one* ever has a right to sex and *everyone* has the right to say no to sex. That goes for kissing, groping and everything else, too. Intimate stuff should only happen when both people want it to. These facts are true no matter what the circumstances.

BEING HOMOPHOBIC (anti-gay)

• If your best friend told you they were gay, would you be put off being friends with them?

• Do you think that being gay is unnatural?

• Do you use words like "bender", "poof", "fag" or "lezzie"?

• If you saw two men or two women kissing in public, would it bother you more than it would seeing a man and woman doing the same thing?

• Is there anything that straight people can do that you think gay people *shouldn't* be allowed to do (like joining a particular profession, adopting children, holding hands in public — anything)?

If you answered yes to two or more of the above, you're prejudiced against gay people, although you may not have even realised it. You probably picked up your ideas from your family, as you were growing up. Now's the time to start thinking for yourself. If you're bright, it's not hard to see the simple truth: everyone is equal, no matter what they get up to in their private lives.

Being Ignorant

• You're alone with someone you're crazy about and you're desperate to shag them, but neither of you has a condom. You might never get a chance like this again. Do you go ahead and do it?

• Do you think that you have little or no chance of getting AIDS, even if you were to have sex without a condom?

• Is it true that if a boy gets very sexually excited, but can't do anything about it, he will be physically damaged in some way?

• Is it true that a girl is safe from the risks of pregnancy and disease during sex if the boy pulls his willy out quickly before he comes?

If you answered yes to any of the above, you know less about sex than you think – and that could spell danger for you and your sex-partners. Being badly informed isn't your fault, but it's up to you to be open-minded and prepared to learn the truth. Read this book very thoroughly!

Chapter Four

GEARING UP FOR SEX

ARE YOU READY TO HAVE SEX?

There's no exact age or time when you suddenly become ready to have sex. It's really about having done just the right amount of growing-up, physically and mentally, and that can happen very early on for some people, and much later for others. The only person who can really tell if you're ready to have sex is you: it's your life, your body and, ultimately, your decision.

Let's answer some of those burning questions...

Surely you're as ready as you feel. Why bother to wonder if you're really ready?
Wanting to have sex is not the same as being ready to have sex, although it's easy to get the two feelings confused. Thinking about it is a good idea, so that you can be *sure* that you're ready, and not get into sexual situations before you are.

What's the big deal about being ready?
It's all about being clued-up and prepared for sex.

If you wait until you're ready, your early experiences should be happy, safe and fulfilling. If you don't, you risk feeling scared and confused and disappointed afterwards. And if you don't know or fully understand the ins-and-outs of sexual protection, you could also end up with an unwanted pregnancy or a nasty disease.

What makes someone ready to have sex?
You need to understand sex and relationships and what you want to get out of them. You need to be able to control your urges and think carefully before rushing into things. You need to know all about sex and safety. In other words, what we're really talking about here is sexual awareness. No one is born sexually aware and, unfortunately, it doesn't just come to you — you have to make it happen. You don't need to have sex to be sexually aware — in fact, the smartest people are sexually aware *long* before they hop into bed with anyone.

SO... HOW SEXUALLY AWARE ARE YOU?

The flow-chart on the following pages was specially devised by a sex-expert to help you find out how sexually aware you are at the moment. Start by answering the first question, following the "yes" or "no" path to the next question, and so on, until you get to one of the four conclusions.

TYPE ONE
You are: Inexperienced — and although some virgins are

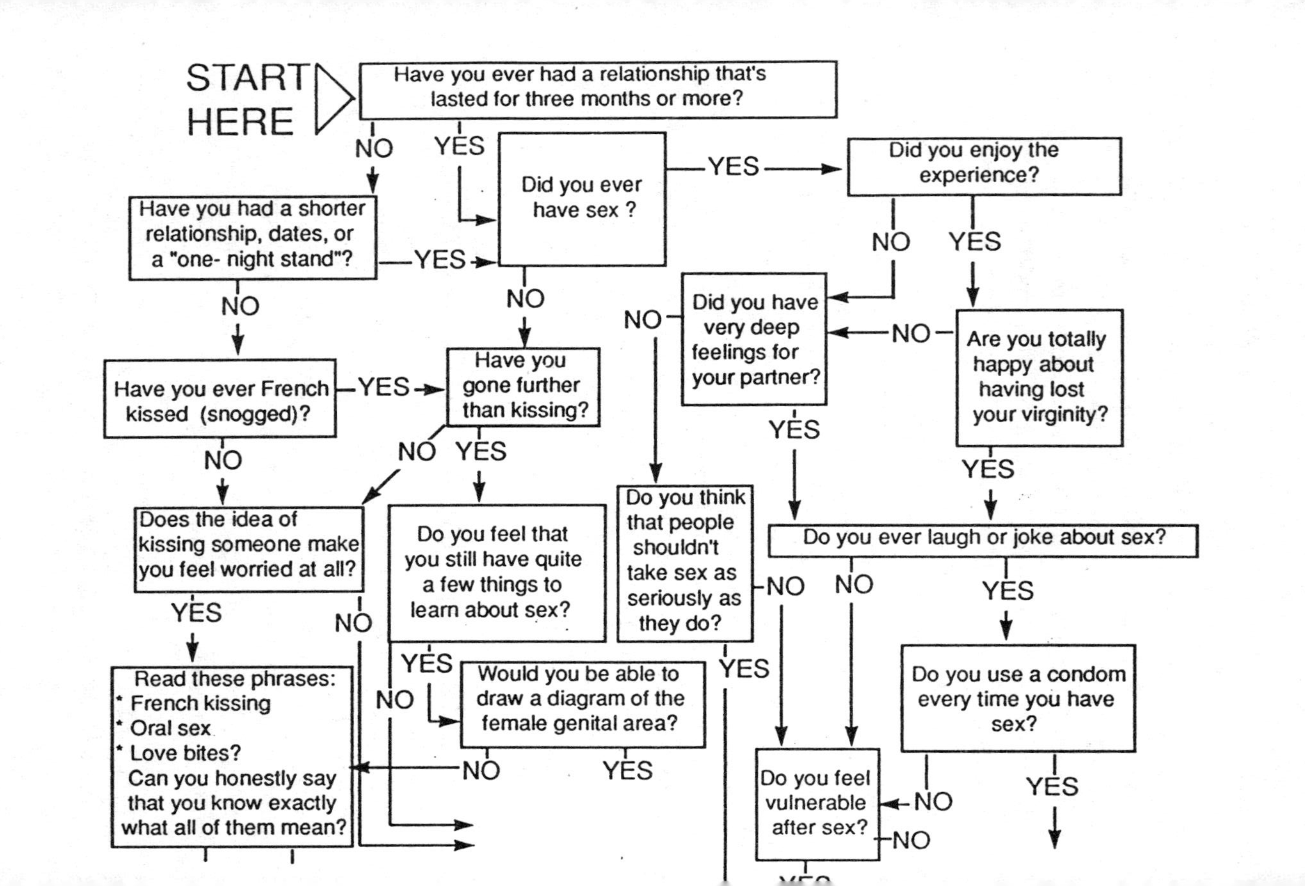

START HERE
Have you ever had a relationship that's lasted for three months or more?
NO
YES
Have you had a shorter relationship, dates, or a "one- night stand"?
YES
NO
Did you ever have sex ?
YES
NO
Did you enjoy the experience?
NO
YES
Have you ever French kissed (snogged)?
YES
NO
Have you gone further than kissing?
NO
YES
Did you have very deep feelings for your partner?
NO
YES
Are you totally happy about having lost your virginity?
NO
YES
Does the idea of kissing someone make you feel worried at all?
YES
NO
Do you feel that you still have quite a few things to learn about sex?
YES
NO
Do you think that people shouldn't take sex as seriously as they do?
NO
YES
Do you ever laugh or joke about sex?
NO
YES
Read these phrases:
* French kissing
* Oral sex
* Love bites?
Can you honestly say that you know exactly what all of them mean?
Would you be able to draw a diagram of the female genital area?
NO
YES
Do you use a condom every time you have sex?
NO
YES
Do you feel vulnerable after sex?
NO

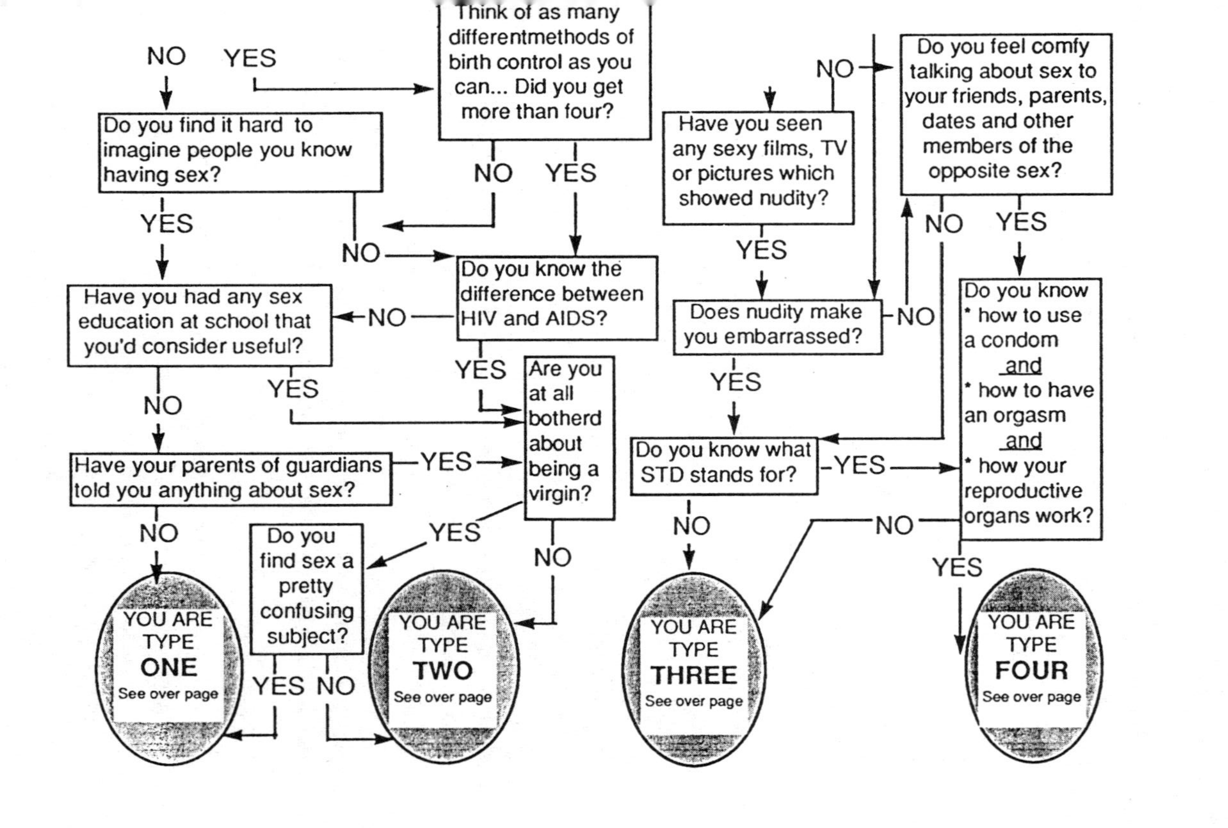
Do you find it hard to imagine people you know having sex?
NO
YES
Think of as many differentmethods of birth control as you can... Did you get more than four?
NO
YES
Do you know the difference between HIV and AIDS?
Have you had any sex education at school that you'd consider useful?
Are you at all botherd about being a virgin?
Have your parents of guardians told you anything about sex?
Do you find sex a pretty confusing subject?
Have you seen any sexy films, TV or pictures which showed nudity?
Does nudity make you embarrassed?
Do you feel comfy talking about sex to your friends, parents, dates and other members of the opposite sex?
Do you know what STD stands for?
Do you know
* how to use a condom
and
* how to have an orgasm
and
* how your reproductive organs work?
YOU ARE TYPE ONE
See over page
YOU ARE TYPE TWO
See over page
YOU ARE TYPE THREE
See over page
YOU ARE TYPE FOUR
See over page

as sexually aware as those who *have* had sexual experiences, you're not one of them. Your knowledge of sexual matters is pretty basic, to say the least. Maybe you're not really interested in sex at the moment — which is fine — or perhaps you find it embarrassing to talk or think about. It seems as if no one has told you anything much about sex — or if they have, you've ignored it, forgotten it, or got the wrong end of the stick.

Try not to: Let your lack of knowledge and understanding of sex worry you or embarrass you — it'll come with a tiny bit of time and effort. However, it's dead important at this stage that you don't decide to find out more by actually getting into a sexual situation with someone — you need to find out and understand quite a bit of stuff on your own first if you want to avoid a potentially nasty experience that could damage you for life.

Try to: Ignore friends who claim to know more and do more, sexually, than you do — the chances are that half of their claims are made-up, and there's no point in comparing yourself to other people anyway. If you want to talk about sex, choose someone older and wiser instead. Whatever you do, read this book thoroughly!

TYPE TWO

You are: A member of a very admirable breed — the smart, clued-up virgin. Although you're very sexually aware, you have chosen not to put your knowledge into practise yet, and you feel pretty happy with your decision. You're obviously interested in sex, as you have clearly gone out of your way to find out and digest lots of important information about it, from all sorts of sources. You might sometimes feel that there are a few things you're not 100% clear on — especially concerning the emotional side of sex and relationships — but you're probably aware that what you know already is plenty for now, and the rest will come in good time.

Try not to: Feel under any pressure to lose your virginity. Your attitude, intelligence and savvy proves that you're a mature person, so you should never feel tempted to rush into sex just to "keep up" with your friends.

Try to: Carry on living in the sensible, grown-up and well-paced way you've been doing already. Wait for someone who you feel is just the right person to share your first sexual experience with — someone bright and wise as you — and you'll be all set for a happy, healthy future sex life.

TYPE THREE

You are: Sexually experienced but not sexually aware — a rather dodgy state to be in. Losing your virginity counts for very little when you don't really understand what you've done or what you're doing. You never gave yourself a chance to understand sex — or what you wanted out of it — before trying it, and the chances are that your experiences haven't been happy or safe.

Try not to: Get any further into deep waters before you've educated yourself some more. Learn as much as you can, as soon as possible. Luckily you've got this

book to help you. Read it carefully and take it all in.
Try to: Get your head together before you have sex again. Feeling more knowledgeable should help, but if you've lost your sense of self respect, you've got to regain it before you risk getting into another sexual situation. If your past experiences have disturbed you, you should try going for counselling. Equally important, you've got to choose more carefully who you have sex with in the future, for your own sake. Whoever it's been so far has either been as much in the dark as you are, or else has been a careless sort who hasn't bothered to get to know you or think about your welfare — either way, not a good choice of partner.

TYPE FOUR
You are: Very sexually aware — not just because of your experience, but because you are well-informed, and able to understand everything you've learnt along the way. You understand a lot about sex, so you aren't afraid of it, and you also have a good, relaxed attitude which means that you feel able to discuss sex honestly and freely with others. In turn, the ability to chat openly about sex helps you to learn more about it.
Try not to: Show off about your sexual knowledge or assume that because you have the sex thing sussed, you also know everything there is to know about relationships. Being sexually aware doesn't mean that you necessarily understand the emotional side of things yet, which can be just as tricky and mystifying as the sexual side.
Try to: Carry on as you are, because you're doing great,

but always be cautious, and open to learning and growing — don't close yourself off by assuming that you know it all already.

SO WHAT AM I WAITING FOR?

Once you're sure that you're ready to cope with sex, and all the complications it can bring into your life, the big questions are when, where and with who? Some people hit this point desperate to "get rid of" their virginity, and don't really care what the circumstances are. This doesn't spell certain disaster, but it's not a great attitude to kick off your sex life with. After all, sex isn't just about *you* — it's a shared experience between two people. If you can wait until exactly the right person comes along, you've got a much better chance of having a happy, fun and safe first time.

These days not many people wait until they're married or engaged, but most agree that it's based on quite a sound wisdom: that if you love and trust someone enough to want to spend a big chunk of your life with them, then they're bound to be a pretty good choice of person to trust your all-important first experience to. Even if you don't plan to wait until you've found a life-long partner (you might not ever want a life-long partner!), it's still a good idea to pick someone you get along with, know well, trust, and want to have a longish relationship with. If you lose your virginity after just a couple of dates — or indeed with someone you just met at a party — there's a good chance that the relationship won't last much past the first bonk. No matter how tough you are, this can be difficult to cope with once you've shared such an intimate experience as sex.

You should never worry about "missing" an opportunity to lose your virginity. It's far better to wait until you're absolutely certain you want to go ahead, than to rush into things and regret it later. If the person you were thinking about having sex with isn't prepared to wait, or give you another chance in the future, then they probably weren't a great bet anyway.

The worst way to lose your virginity is when you're so drunk or out of it that you don't know what's going on. If you deliberately get blotto because you're nervous about sex, then you're not really ready, and should wait until the prospect seems less terrifying. If you have sex because you're not in any fit state to make a decision one way or another, then your partner is taking advantage of you and is probably a grade-A sod who doesn't deserve you in the first place. The answer is either to avoid excessive drinking or taking drugs in situations where you might do something you regret, or to make sure that your friends keep an eye on you and are prepared to stuff you in a taxi or drag you home before you can do anything.

IS NOW THE RIGHT TIME?

If you're considering taking a relationship further — i.e.

having sex — not just for the first time, but any time, you should always ask yourself these questions:

• Do I *really* like, fancy, care about or maybe even love my prospective partner?

• Do they like, fancy, care about or maybe even love me, too?

• If I don't feel like I want to have sex now, would my partner be prepared to wait until I do?

• Am I certain that my partner is okay about us using a condom?

• Have I or my partner got a condom already, or is one of us prepared to go out and buy some before we decide to have sex?

Now ask yourself these:

• Is there any possibility that my partner is "just after one thing" and might dump me afterwards?

• Has my partner ever put me under any pressure to go further than I really wanted to?

• Has my partner ever threatened or implied that they might leave me if I don't have sex?

• If my partner *had* threatened to leave me if I wouldn't

have sex, would I go ahead and have sex anyway, even if I didn't want to?

• Is wanting to "keep up" with my friends an important factor in my decision?

• Is wanting to "get rid of" my virginity an important factor?

If you answered a definite "yes" to all of the first set of questions and a definite "no" to all the questions in the second set, then you're onto a winner. You've got all the ingredients for a happy, safe sexual experience, and should feel free to start as soon as you feel like it!

If you answered "no" to any of the questions in the first section, or "yes" to any in the second, put the brakes on. The chances are that things will turn out fine, but you need to think things through and get to know your partner better first.

If you have sex for dodgy reasons, with a dodgy person or without taking precautions against pregnancy and disease, you're not doing yourself any favours, to say the least. Not only could you end up miserable, confused or worse, but you're also sending an invisible message to your partner — and the rest of the world — that says: "Hello! I don't think I'm worth much! Look at me — I don't care what happens to me! Feel free to use me, why don't you!" People with that attitude spend their whole lives being used, abused, stepped on and generally made miserable by everyone else. Choosing the right time to have sex is really all about having self-respect — the most important thing anyone can have.

What if I don't get a chance to think carefully before I have sex?
That happens. You might be in a very intimate situation — alone with someone, having a heavy, passionate snogging and petting session and suddenly you realise that you're on the verge of losing your virginity. In these cases, you just have to go with your gut instinct — do you *really* want to do it? Not because all your friends have, not because you're scared of losing your partner, not because you figure you "might as well" now you're this close to it, nor because you're worried about being a "tease" if you back out, but because you *really, really* want to experience sex and closeness with this person, *right* now? If the answer is a definite yes, then as long as one of you has a condom ready to use, there's no reason why you shouldn't go ahead.

LOSING YOUR VIRGINITY

No matter how aware or well-prepared you are, everyone worries just a bit about their first time. Here are some of the most common frets...
Can someone tell if you're a virgin?
Not by looking at you, no.

What about during sex?
Not necessarily. Boys have no physical signs of virginity at all. The only physical sign of virginity for girls is the hymen — a thin piece of skin that grows across the entrance to the vagina. Not all girls still have theirs when they come to have sex for the first time. If they do, it can feel like a sort of barrier. It breaks quite easily and sometimes bleeds a little bit. If the girl's partner notices this (which he might not) then he *would* know she was a virgin. However, most girls' hymens break before they lose their virginity, usually without them even knowing it. This can be caused by a thousand things, including putting something in the vagina (like a tampon) or doing something physical that involves stretching your legs apart — like horse riding, bike-riding, climbing a tree, doing gymnastics or, in the case of the author, sitting on a toilet backwards at the age of six!

Couldn't someone tell that you were inexperienced?
Yes perhaps. If your partner had had sex in the past with someone who was experienced, and someone else who wasn't, they might be able to make a comparison and tell the difference. Inexperienced boys often come more quickly, although many experienced boys — and men — come quickly too, so it's not a foolproof sign. Inexperienced girls usually move around less and seem more inhibited and shy than experienced ones — though, again, the same goes for some experienced females. But even if someone could tell that you were inexperienced, they wouldn't know if you were

a virgin or not.

If you don't want your partner to know that you're a virgin, you should ask yourself why not. If you're in a loving relationship, then your partner should be flattered, nay overjoyed, that you've chosen them to be the very, very special person who shares your first sexual experience. If you really don't like the idea of them knowing, then perhaps they're not a great choice of partner. After all, if you don't feel comfortable enough to tell them something that important, how the heck are you going to feel relaxed enough to enjoy sex with them?

I don't like using tampons, and when I've tried putting my fingers inside myself, more than one hurts and feels too big... I'm worried that my vagina will be too small to fit a willy inside it...

Don't worry. It's virtually unheard of for a girl's fanny to be too small for sex. We're talking about a remarkably stretchy organ, that can comfortably expand to fit any willy, no matter how long or wide it is. Just remember, a vagina can stretch enough to let a baby out — and no boy on the planet has a willy the size of a baby, anyway! Some boys like to brag by warning girls that their willy might be "too big" for them. This is a load of old guff — ignore it.

Does losing your virginity hurt?

It varies. Most boys and many girls find it doesn't hurt at all. Most girls and a few boys find that it hurts just a little bit when the willy first goes in, but then it's absolutely fine. Some girls find the whole thing quite painful. Both boys and girls can feel a little bit sore afterwards.

Generally, though, losing your virginity never hurts enough to put you off sex!

Is there anything you can do to make it hurt less?
Yep, several things. Firstly, it's worth knowing that the more damp the vagina is, the easier and less painful it is for the willy to slip in. If a girl is happy, relaxed and sexually excited she makes her own natural *lubrication* (wetness). This is what people mean when they talk about a girl *getting wet*. If your condom comes ready-lubricated (with spermicide or lubricant) this helps too. You can also buy lubricants from the chemist — just be sure to choose one such as KY jelly that doesn't weaken your condom. It can also be more painful if the girl is tensing up all the muscles in her fanny — another reason why it's important for the girl to feel relaxed. If you can't relax, it's still possible to relax your vaginal muscles if you concentrate!

Will my partner enjoy having sex with me if I'm a virgin and I don't know what to do?
If you're both virgins, then at least you won't have to worry about being compared to any of your partner's previous conquests. If your partner isn't a virgin, though, it still shouldn't make any difference to them. For a start, a lot of girls and boys find the idea of being

the first person to make love to someone else very ego-boosting and sexy. Secondly, if they care about you, then they're having sex to get closer to you, so they'll enjoy it whatever happens. Bear in mind too, that they fancy you and will be very turned on by seeing and feeling your body and getting close to you, so it's going to be neither here nor there if you're not swinging from the light fitments or practising strange ancient eastern sexual rituals.

Will I enjoy losing my virginity?
Hopefully! It's unlikely that the earth will move, fireworks will go off and you'll suddenly think: "A-ha! So this is what all the fuss is about!", because those feelings usually come when you're *really* comfortable with your partner, your own body and having sex. That said, experiencing the magical closeness of sex with someone you really like can be — and should be — wonderful from the word go, and if you're lucky, it'll be very sexually exciting too. If you're a girl, you can't expect definitely to have an orgasm — but hopefully it'll be a really pleasurable experience anyway. The after-effects of losing your virginity can be very nice too — you feel closer to your partner and more worldly. Most adults agree, looking back, that their first sexual experience is never their best, but most enjoy it tons, anyway... And isn't it nice to know that it just keeps getting better and better?

Chapter Five

THINK BEFORE YOU BONK

Let's get a handful of facts straight right away:

1) Getting a sexually transmitted disease (STD) is no fun at all, and can be very serious.

2) An unwanted pregnancy can ruin your life.

3) The AIDS virus ruins your life and then kills you.

If you have sex, you risk getting an STD - including AIDS - getting pregnant or getting someone else pregnant unless you take proper precautions.

You'll find everything you need to know about STDs later on, in Chapter Eight. This chapter is all about AIDS and pregnancy. If you think you know it all already, you could be wrong. Read it anyway.

PREGNANCY

Pregnancy happens when a sperm meets up with a ripe

female egg. You don't have to be a genius to work out that it's pretty easy to get pregnant, especially if you know the facts:

- Every time a boy comes, he sets free literally *millions* of sperm.

- A girl releases just one egg a month, but it's ripe to be fertilised (joined by a sperm) for between one and three days.

- It's nearly impossible for a girl to tell exactly when her eggs are released.

- Sperm can live inside a girl for ages — five days is quite normal — so even if there's no ripe egg on the day that a girl has sex, there could still be plenty of sperm about when it finally turns up.

There is only one way that you can have sex and be sure that pregnancy doesn't happen: using a proper method of *contraception* (also known as *birthcontrol* or *protection*). That's it. There's no way around it. If you don't make the effort to get birthcontrol sorted out, you could end up with an unwanted pregnancy.

There are plenty of myths about how you can avoid pregnancy without using birth control. Some are based on misunderstandings of the truth, others are just utter crap invented by cretins. Perhaps you've heard you can't get pregnant if:
...It's your first time

...Your partner masturbates before having sex
...You have sex standing up
...You don't have an orgasm
...You jump up and down a lot afterwards
...You wee afterwards
...You have a bath afterwards
...You wash your fanny out with a fizzy cola drink afterwards
These are all pretty silly, but they've stuck around for years and years because people go on believing them, and telling their friends all about them. If people can believe those, then it's no surprise that they also buy the myths which sound quite logical and sensible. How about:

• *The safe time* — the belief that a girl can't get pregnant during her period. Although a girl is less likely to get pregnant during her period, it's by no means impossible. Don't risk it.

• *Douching* — you might have seen douches in the chemists. They're bags of liquid with a tube on the end that you use to clean inside the vagina. Some people believe that if you use one right after sex, it flushes all the sperm out, and therefore protects you against pregnancy. This is crap, and in actual fact, douching after sex can help shove the sperm up further, making pregnancy even more likely. Besides this, douching can be quite bad for you, so there's no reason to even consider trying this dumb trick.

• *The withdrawal method*, also known as *being careful* — the belief that if a boy pulls his willy out before he comes, his partner can't get pregnant because the semen doesn't go inside her. What's so scary about this is that *so many* people — adults included — think that it's true, when it's actually complete nonsense. In fact, a little bit of semen — known as *pre-ejaculate* — almost always sneaks out long before the big spurt happens. It's usually an amount so small that you wouldn't notice it, but the scary truth is that this weeny bit of spunk contains loads of sperm.

All that brings us back to square one. There's simply no alternative to using birth control. So what kind of contraception should you use? There's certainly lots of choice, but before we check it out, there's another very important thing to consider. These days you don't just need to protect against pregnancy...

AIDS

If you're having sex, you're at risk of getting AIDS. Despite many years of research, scientists still don't know everything there is to know about it. Luckily, though, they've already found out enough for us to be able to protect ourselves. Here are the bare facts:

• AIDS stands for *Acquired Immune Deficiency Syndrome*, and it's a fatal disease — in other words if you have it, you will almost definitely die.

• AIDS is caused by a virus called HIV, which stands for *Human Immunodeficiency Virus.* People who are infected with this virus usually go on to develop AIDS.

• There is no cure for HIV or AIDS, and no vaccination that can protect you from them.

• You catch the HIV virus from other people who are infected with it.

• It's impossible to tell who has got it and who hasn't, because people infected with HIV don't seem ill, feel ill or look any different from anyone else until they start to develop AIDS. This can happen as long as ten years after getting infected.

• *Anyone* can get infected by the HIV virus. You don't have to be gay, a drug-user or anything else.

• People carry the HIV virus in their blood and other body fluids, like semen and vaginal juices.

• When you have sex, you and your partner come into contact with one another's fluids. If one of you has HIV, the other could get infected.

• The only way to help protect yourself and your partner is to use a condom when you have sex.

Even though almost everyone has heard about AIDS, there's still lots of stuff that people are unsure about.

Let's get some answers...

Is it easy to catch HIV?
If you're not having sex, you're at very little risk, so don't panic. Just remember:

• You can't catch the virus from an infected person by touching them, shaking hands or holding hands with them, hugging or kissing.

• You can't catch the virus from using things an infected person has used (like phones, headphones, books, soap or towels), sitting where they've sat (including on toilets), wearing clothes they've worn, using the same shower or swimming pool or sharing things like food, knives and forks, plates, cups and make-up.

• You can't catch the virus from an infected person breathing, sneezing or coughing near you.

So you can only catch it from having sex?
Well, no. You catch the HIV virus when an infected person's bodily fluids enter your body, and there *are* ways this can happen that don't involve sex. The good news is that these risks are quite easily avoided:

• If an infected person was bleeding and you also happened to have an open wound — even a scratch or small cut — there would be a chance that some of their blood could enter your bloodstream if you touched them. If someone is bleeding, be careful.

• If you have to clean up someone else's blood, always wear rubber gloves to protect yourself.

• If you're a drug-user who injects drugs (an *intravenous drug-user*) and you shared a needle with an infected person, you would run a very high risk of getting infected. Even if you cleaned the needle first, some of their blood would still be there, and it would go directly into your bloodstream. The only way a drug-user can stay safe is always to use a fresh needle and syringe.

• If you ever find a syringe or needle lying around, don't touch it — it could be infected.

• Anything that has had blood on it is a potential hazard. If you are considering having a tattoo, acupuncture or electrolysis, or getting your ears pierced, you should always check that the equipment has been properly sterilised before it is used on you. Don't be afraid to ask — reputable acupuncturists, tattooists and beauticians are very careful about hygiene and will understand perfectly why you want to know. If they get funny, go somewhere else — it's not worth the risk.

• It's not a good idea to share a toothbrush or wet-shave

razor with anyone, because of the risk of blood from bleeding gums or shaving cuts.

What about having a blood transfusion? Isn't that dangerous?
When AIDS was first discovered, it turned out, tragically, that many people had been infected by HIV through getting blood transfusions in hospital, or other medical treatments that involved products made of blood. These days, though, all blood in this country and most of the foreign countries you'd be likely to visit for a holiday, is screened for the HIV virus before it can be used, so you don't need to worry about it.

If you had sex with someone who was infected with HIV, would you definitely catch it?
Not definitely, but the risk would be very high. When you have sex without wearing a condom, the boy's semen gets into the girl's fanny, and the girl's vaginal juices get all over the boy's willy. If someone is infected with HIV, their juices will be full of the virus. Work it out for yourself...

But hold on, I thought that the virus had to actually get into your blood? How the heck does that happen in sex?
It can happen in several ways. Let's look at the girl's body first.

• It's quite normal for the skin on the inside of a girl's vagina to have tiny little tears in it. These are usually caused by having sex, although you can also get them from using a tampon or having an internal examination at the doctors. These tears don't hurt when you get them, or afterwards (so you'll never know that they're there). They can take ages to heal, and if you're having sex regularly, they might not get a chance, because they'll keep getting reopened. A boy's semen goes into these little gaps in the skin, and into the girl's bloodstream — very bad news if he's got HIV.

• The skin on a boy's willy also gets little tears in it during sex, or even wanking. They don't hurt and are usually too small to see, so, again, you won't know they're there. During sex, the girl's vaginal juices get onto the willy, through these little abrasions and into the boy's bloodstream. If her juices are carrying the HIV virus, he's at risk.

• A girl's fluids can also get into a boy's bloodstream during sex through the little hole in the end of the willy. This is the urethra (the tube that leads to the bladder) and it doesn't usually let things into the body — if it did you wouldn't be able to have a bath without getting your willy full of water! During sex, though, the in-and-out action can create a kind of vacuum, and work like a pump, drawing fluid into the urethra.

• If a girl is having her period when she has sex, the boy would absorb her menstrual blood as well as her vaginal fluids. Blood carries more of the HIV virus than other fluids, so he would have an even higher risk of his catching it if she had it.

• Anal sex (where a boy puts his willy inside a girl or boy's bum) is extra-risky for both partners. A bum-hole almost always has tears inside it from straining when you poo, so the owner of the bum is always at risk. Because the anal passage is narrower and less stretchy than a vagina, and doesn't make any natural lubrication, putting a willy inside it can tear it quite a lot more — often enough to make it bleed a tiny bit. The willy usually gets extra abrasions during anal sex too, so it's a big risk for the owner of the willy, too - his partner's blood can get into these tears.

• Penetrative sex — where the willy goes into the fanny or bum — is known as a *high-risk activity.*

So is non-penetrative sex low-risk?
It depends what you do. For instance:

• Anything you do which could end up with sperm, vaginal fluid or period-blood getting into someone's vagina or bum or onto their willy is risky. This would include touching your own privates before touching your partner's or sharing a sex toy like a vibrator or dildo with someone else is also high risk. (If you don't know what these are, turn to Chapter Nine).

• Oral sex (where you kiss, lick or suck your partner's privates) is a low to medium-risk activity. It's technically possible to get HIV like this, especially if the person performing the deed has cracked lips, cut gums, mouth ulcers, or little abrasions inside their mouth that they don't even know about. The owner of the mouth is at more risk than their partner, and mouth-to-willy oral sex is more dangerous than mouth-to-fanny oral sex, because if the boy comes in your mouth, his semen could get into any of the little openings mentioned above. There aren't many proven cases of people catching HIV through oral sex, but many AIDS experts recommend using a condom for oral sex with a boy anyway. The majority of people go without those things and take the risk — it's not necessarily the most sensible thing, but that's the way it is.

• Some experts say that French kissing is a low-risk activity, others say that it's not risky at all. Although traces of the HIV virus have been found in saliva, it's nowhere near as concentrated as it is in other fluids, so it'd take bucketloads to put you at any risk at all. It's wildly unlikely — if not impossible — that you could catch HIV this way.

How would you know if you had caught HIV?
You wouldn't, because you wouldn't get ill until you developed full-blown AIDS, and it can be many years before that happens. The only way to tell if you've been infected with HIV is to go for a special blood test. Here

are the facts about it:

• You can get advice and info about having an AIDS test from clinics that specialise in sexually transmitted diseases (known as STD clinics), or by calling an AIDS advisory help line (you'll find some numbers in the back of this book).

• If you decide to have a test, the best place to go is an STD clinic. Your GP can do it too, but people generally prefer clinics because they are faster, and you don't have to tell them your name or anything about yourself if you don't want to.

• The test works by looking for antibodies to the HIV virus in your blood — that is, disease-fighting proteins that your body has made to try and fight off the virus. It can take anything up to three months after infection for your body to make these antibodies, so it would be pointless to rush off and have a test a week after having unprotected sex, because the result would probably be negative even if you were infected. Always wait until at least three months after unprotected sex before having an AIDS test.

• Before you actually have the test, a clinic will give you counselling. That means they'll talk to you all about the test and give you a chance to chat about how you feel.

• It usually takes from two days to a couple of weeks to get your results, depending on where you go as the test is quite long and involved. Some clinics offer same-day results which is good because you'll have less time to worry.

• Most clinics will give you your result face to face, in private. If the test has discovered that you are HIV positive (which means that you have the HIV virus), you won't just be sent off to deal with the news alone. The clinic will give you proper counselling and help you arrange what to do next.

Like what?

You'd sign up with a specialist doctor who would give you medical information, and an AIDS counsellor who would help you come to terms with your illness and put you in touch with support groups.

Medically, there isn't much you can do. Up until recently, many people with HIV started taking medication right away, hoping it might help prevent the onset of AIDS. Unfortunately these drugs are still in the experimental stages, and many experts now believe that they do more harm than good. Still, many people try and improve their chances of staying healthy for longer by eating well, keeping fit and giving up drinking and smoking. Others have very good things to say about alternative medicines and therapies, like reflexology, acupuncture and homeopathy.

So why would anyone want to know if they had a fatal

disease if there was no cure for it?
Most people would rather know the truth just to put their mind at rest — after all, wouldn't it be a huge relief to find out you were clear? Even if you'd rather not know, shouldn't you have a test for the sake of your family, friends and sexual partners? If you had the HIV virus and didn't know about it you could risk infecting them. Knowing that you are infected gives you the chance to take extra precautions.

I asked about an AIDS test but my doctor said that if I wasn't gay and didn't inject drugs I probably didn't need one...
Unfortunately, even doctors can be ignorant. It's been true that intravenous drug users, people who sleep with them, gay and bisexual men who have anal sex and women who sleep with them have always had a greater chance of catching AIDS than anyone else. However, anyone can catch AIDS, and the cases of straight, drug-free people with AIDS is growing all the time — probably due to people mistakenly thinking they're not at any risk.

The only way to stay safe is to use a condom *every time* you have sex.

CONDOMS

Condoms, also known as *sheaths, rubbers, Durex, French letters, johnnies* and *willy covers,* are a rather brilliant invention. They're inexpensive, small and easy to carry around and they're the key to being able to have sex without playing Russian roulette with your life. A condom is a willy-shaped tube made of very thin latex rubber, and it keeps the boy's semen in and everything else out, so both the wearer and his partner are protected. If you or your partner are allergic to rubber, you can get special condoms — ask your doctor or local Family Planning Clinic about them.

How do you use a condom?

Condoms come in little, square individual wrappers. When you take the condom out of this, it's all rolled up very tightly, so that it looks like a little circle with a raised ring round the edge, and a small bobble in the middle. Don't unroll it! Here's how to put one on properly:

- Hold the condom by the tip (the bobble in the middle), squeezing out any air that might be in it, and place it on the end of the willy.

- Gently place your thumb and forefinger on either side of the raised ring round the edge, and start rolling the whole thing down. You can use your other hand to help, if you need to. If it won't roll easily, it's on upside down — start again.

- Always unroll a condom carefully, being careful not to tear it, especially if you've got long nails. Once the condom is completely unrolled, and feels perfectly snug, you're ready to rock!

Should the boy put it on himself?
Not necessarily. His partner could do it, or they could do it together. Actually, lots of couples find that putting on a condom is a sexy, nice experience, and see it as a part of love-making.

Is it difficult to put on a condom?
Not really — and the more you do it, the easier it gets. It's a good idea to get some condoms to practise with *before* you have sex, because the more confident you are with them, the less chance there is of having an embarrassing, fumbling experience when it comes to the real thing. If you're a boy, you've already got all the equipment you need to practise. If you're a girl, practise putting one on a carrot, banana or candle, or just a couple of your fingers. If you've used a condom for practising, chuck it out afterwards: it's no good for sex once it's been unrolled and fiddled with.

Someone told me that you can put a condom on with your mouth. Is that true?
Yes, a boy's partner can do this as a bit of sexy fun! It takes practise, but the general idea is to unwrap the condom, place it just behind your teeth with the tip facing inwards, then open wide and plonk it onto your

partner's willy. Once it's sitting there safely, you can start unrolling by pressing your lips together just above the raised ring and slowly lowering your mouth down the shaft. Don't choke yourself – you can finish the job with your tongue!

When should you put a condom on?
After the boy's willy has become erect, but long before it goes anywhere near his partner's bits!

When should you take it off again?
Straightaway after the boy has come, while his willy is still quite hard – otherwise the condom could go loose enough to leak semen out, or actually come off inside his partner.

Which condom should I buy?
The most important thing to look for when you're choosing is safety and quality. If a packet of condoms has the British Standards Authority "kite mark" on it, that means it's been through tough testing and is top quality. You can also be sure that you're onto a safe bet if you choose condoms made by a well-known company like Durex, Mates or Jiffi.

You'll see lots of different types of condom, with all sorts of strange names and descriptions, including brightly- coloured ones (a bit of fun) and flavoured ones (not a bad idea if you're using them for oral sex or want to try putting them on with your mouth, as most regular condoms taste gross). There's no "best" type of condom — it's a matter of personal taste, and most people try a few different ones before settling with one they like. As a rough guide, though, many boys prefer ultra-thin ones (sometimes called "gossamer") because they say they can feel more, and it's also very smart to go for a condom that is coated with a spermicide called Nonoxynol 9. Spermicide is a chemical that kills sperm (in case any escape!), and it also gives extra protection from HIV and other sexually transmitted diseases (see Chapter Eight for more about those). If you pick condoms without spermicide, you might want to buy some spermicide to use with them, for extra protection. Spermicide also makes a good lubricant — that is, it helps the willy slip in more easily and can make sex more comfortable. While we're on the subject of lubricants, it's important to know that most household or beauty products (such as oils or creams) are a total no-no: they can weaken or dissolve the condom. If you want a lubricant that's not a spermicide, get one that's been designed for the job, such as KY Jelly.

Where do I buy all this stuff?

You'll find spermicide, lubricant and a huge range of condoms at your local chemist or pharmacy, usually near the till. Most high street chemists now place the condoms in easy reach of customers, so you shouldn't have to ask for them.

You'll also probably find condoms in supermarkets (with the toiletries) or at general stores, corner shops and mini-markets (normally at the till). Many high street fashion shops, chain stores and hairdressers sell condoms too. You can also find dispensing machines in the toilets and hallways of most pubs, restaurants, youth clubs, cinemas and leisure centres.

Many people don't realise that their local Family Planning Clinic can supply condoms if you go in for a consultation. The great news is that they're absolutely free! You can find the address of your nearest centre in the phone book, or call the Family Planning Association (you'll find the number in the back of this book).

What if I'm too embarrassed to buy condoms?

If you're not embarrassed to have sex, then there's no reason why you should be embarrassed to buy condoms. Just go into a shop, look for them, pick up a packet and pay. It's no more embarrassing than buying batteries, tissues or anything else, and no one is going to ask you any questions. Or why not get them from a dispensing machine? You can always wait until there's no one else around.

When should I buy condoms?

Well before you get an opportunity to use them! You don't have to be certain that you're going to have sex to buy condoms. It's better to buy them just in case and hang on to them for a bit than to be caught short. If you feel ready to have sex, and you're going out on dates where you hope very much that you'll be lucky, it's time to get yourself some condoms. If you're in a steady relationship and you seem to be going a little bit further every time you get together, it's *definitely* time. Keep at least one wrapped condom in the bag or jacket you use regularly, and at least one in your room. Condoms have a long shelf-life, so don't worry if they just sit gathering dust for a while — you're bound to use them eventually, and you'll be ever so glad you had them.

Do people think that a girl who carries a condom is "easy"?
Anyone with half a brain would think that a girl who carried a condom was very mature and smart. Anyone who thinks otherwise is a prat, and not worth worrying about.

I'd like to keep some condoms just in case, but I'm scared of my parents finding them...
Some parents would indeed throw a wobbly if they discovered your condoms, because they'd assume that you were having sex, and be put out that they didn't know anything about it.

Hopefully, though, once they got over the shock, they'd feel relieved that you were taking all the proper precautions and go easy on you. If your parents are easy-going, you could try talking to them about your plans — then you wouldn't have to worry about being found out. If you really can't talk to them, then you'll just have to hide the condoms very well. Whatever, don't let the fear of being found out put you off. Your safety is the most important thing, and it's better to have condoms and risk a parental strop than not to have them at all.

When should I mention condoms to my partner?
If you're in a proper relationship and you've talked about having sex, or are actually planning it, then it's obviously a close, mature relationship and you can mention condoms when you're chatting. If you're not that relaxed with your partner yet, but it looks like you're going to have sex anyway, you should take the initiative. First, make sure you've got a condom handy in case your partner hasn't. Wait until you're pretty sure that sex is on the cards, but not so late that there's no turning back. If you're on your own, with no chance of being disturbed, you've been snogging or petting for a while, one or both of you have shed a few items of clothing, and whoever's got the willy has an erection, then it's definitely time to stop and mention condoms.

But what do I say?
You could start with a simple, friendly, "Wait a minute...", then say, "Do you think I should get a condom for us?" Alternatively, stop and get the condom out, then say, "I think I should put this on..." or "I think you should put this on..." It all sounds rather scary, because it's a bit like saying, "Okay, it's shagging time!"

and there's always the teeny weeny chance that your partner wasn't planning to go that far. It doesn't really matter, though — at least you've made it clear that when you eventually have sex, you won't do it without a condom. If your partner is bright, they'll be relieved — it was probably on their mind too.

What if my partner doesn't like condoms?

If someone refuses to wear a condom, or says they don't want you to wear one, it's time to stop and think long and hard about that person and your relationship with them. Refusing to use a condom is like saying, "I don't care about you and your safety, and I don't care about myself, either." Do you really want to share your affections and your body with someone who is that stupid and thoughtless? Even if you fancy them like crazy, or you're terrified that you'll lose them if you make a fuss, it's not worth it. You've got to stand up for yourself and your safety. If you show your partner that you respect yourself enough to put your foot down over this, they'll respect you back. If you give in on such an important issue, your partner will know that he or she can get away with treating you like a doormat.

What if I don't like condoms?

There probably isn't a person in the world who actually prefers sex with a condom to sex without. Some boys complain that their willy doesn't feel quite as sensitive with one on, and not many people particularly like stopping whatever they're doing to put one on. But any intelligent person should realise that there's no choice. It would be a lovely feeling if you could go scuba diving without having to wear goggles and an oxygen tank, but no one would try it, because wearing diving gear is a far better option than drowning, isn't it? The same goes for condoms. They're not that much hassle, they don't make that much difference to how sex feels (most people find they make no difference at all) and using one is a tiny, tiny price to pay for peace of mind. When you're wearing a condom, you can just relax and enjoy yourself — what could be better than that?

What happens if I get into a situation where I wasn't expecting to have sex, and we don't have any condoms?
Don't have sex! You could always do "everything but" — like snog, cuddle, play with each other and maybe even have oral sex. If you feel like you might get carried away, though, and not be able to resist the lure of actual shagging, then do something else entirely — watch telly, eat something, go for a walk, whatever. Then make a date for tomorrow night that you can both look forward to — and decide who's going to bring the condoms!

Remember: if you always carry a condom, you'll never get into that situation!

Can you re-use a condom?
No. Condoms are designed to be chucked out after one use. In a total emergency, though, a used condom that's

been carefully washed, dried and checked over for tears is better than no condom at all... But waiting until you've got a fresh condom would be better still.

I've seen adverts for a female condom. What is it?
Not long ago a new product came onto the market called the Femidom, which is a condom that girls wear. It gives the same protection against disease and pregnancy as a condom, and it works roughly the same way. A Femidom is a long, slim tube of latex rubber that's slightly wider than a condom, and much wider at the open end. Instead of going over a willy, it goes inside a girl's vagina.

Femidoms are a top-notch invention, because a girl can carry one and use one without having to feel that she's putting any pressure on her partner to do anything. They haven't really caught on in a big way yet — perhaps because people aren't used to them and think they're a bit funny, or maybe because they're worried that they might not be able to use them properly. It's great to have an alternative to male condoms. Why not give them a try?

Is there any time when it's safe to have sex without using a condom or Femidom?
There are some circumstances where you could be pretty sure that you weren't at risk from HIV. Even so, you wouldn't be safe from the risk of pregnancy. If you don't wear a condom or Femidom, and you don't want

to make a baby, you'll need to use some other form of contraception. These are the circumstances where you wouldn't need to worry about HIV:

• If you and your partner are both virgins, and have never shared a needle for drugs, you both have a high chance of being disease-free. This means you don't have to worry about passing anything on to each other. However, you have to be 100 per cent sure that your partner is telling the truth about their history. It's really a question of trust, and you're actually trusting your partner with your life — so you'd have to be really certain.

• If you and your partner had both had AIDS tests which proved you were HIV negative you could be fairly sure that you were safe — as long as neither of you had slept (or shared a needle) with anyone else for at least three months before you had the test or slept (or shared a needle) with anyone else since. Many people in steady relationships who plan to stay together for a long time in the future take AIDS tests so that they can stop using condoms.

CONTRACEPTION

If you're being clever, and using a condom or Femidom to protect yourself against AIDS, you're also reducing the risk of pregnancy. They're a fairly reliable form of birth control, but not *the* most reliable. Both can split or tear, letting sperm through. If the boy doesn't take his willy out right away after he's come, sperm can leak out. And condoms can come off inside a girl when her partner withdraws. If you use a spermicide as well, the risk of pregnancy is slightly lower, even if you have an accident, but even so, many doctors insist that it's a good idea to use some other form of contraception, too, as back-up.

There are quite a lot of different methods of birth control available, but apart from condoms, all of them are designed to be used by girls. Despite this, many people think that contraception should be the responsibility of *both* partners. It's true to an extent — a bloke should never assume that birth control is not his responsibility, and he owes it to his girlfriend to give her any help and support she wants where birth control is concerned. Having said that, it's the girl who actually has to use the contraception and put up with any side-effects, so it should really be up to her which method she uses. Here's what's available:

The Pill

The pill is a little tablet containing hormones that stop you from getting pregnant — either by preventing you from releasing eggs, or by making a special, thick mucus in the entrance to your womb which acts as a barrier to sperm.

There are two main kinds of pill — one that you take every day for three weeks out of every four, with a break for your period (the *combined pill*), and another that you take 365 days a year, at the same time every day (the *mini-pill*). Both come in sheets containing enough pills for a month. When you're given the pill, never leave the doctor's office until you're 100 per cent sure that you understand how and when to take it. If you do it wrong, it won't work. Also be sure that the doctor warns you of other factors that can stop the pill from working (such as antibiotics, diarrohea, and being sick).

Advantages: If you use it properly, it's very, very reliable. In fact it's one of the most reliable methods you can use.

Disadvantages: You have to remember to take a pill every day, and if you forget one, you have to use another method of contraception for a while until you're protected again (you should always check with your doctor to find out exactly how long, because it varies depending on which pill you take). There are also possible side-effects, like weight-gain, headaches, achy bosoms, vaginal infections, depression, moodiness, feeling sleepy and feeling sick. Not everyone gets side-effects, though, and sometimes just changing to a different brand of pill can make the problem go away. However, the pill is also believed to increase the risk of getting heart disease, high blood-pressure and other serious conditions. If you smoke, or have a history of certain illnesses in your family, you're at even more risk, so you should always have a good chat with your doctor about your habits and medical background before going on the pill. Apart from the side-effects and risks, some girls and women just don't like the pill because they don't like the idea of interfering with their bodies' natural hormone balance.

Other Hormone Methods

There are other methods that work the same way as the pill. One is hormone injections, which you get given by your doctor. They keep you protected for several months at a time. There's also a new method fresh over from the USA which is a tiny device that gets implanted in your upper arm, under anaesthetic. It releases enough hormones to keep you protected from pregnancy for several years, but it can be removed if you decide you want to have a baby before it runs out.

Advantages: Once you've been injected, or given the implant, you don't have to worry or even think about contraception. These methods are also very, very reliable — they are technically as reliable as the pill, and probably even more reliable in practise — you don't have to remember to take them every day, so you can't make a mistake.

Disadvantages: Both methods have all the same drawbacks as the pill (apart from having to remember to take it every day of course).

The Diaphragm

A diaphragm, also known as a *cap*, or *Dutch cap*, is a

little, shallow, dome-shaped thing made of thin rubber — though if you're allergic to rubber, you can get one made of plastic. You cover it with spermicide and slip it into your vagina, where it fits over the entrance to your womb. It needs to be put in before you have sex (anything up to three hours before is okay), then left in for at least six hours afterwards. Neither you nor your partner can feel it at all. It works simply by blocking the way in for unwanted sperm, but sperm are sneaky little blighters, which is why you need to use spermicide for extra protection!

Advantages: It is easy to put in once you've had a couple of goes, and with spermicide it's pretty reliable — not as reliable as the pill, but just as good as the condom or Femidom. And remember, if you're using a condom as well, for protection against disease, it's very unlikely that both methods would go wrong at the same time. The cap is also quite a nice, natural method that doesn't interfere with your body's natural workings and hormone balance like the pill and other hormone methods do.

Disadvantages: You have to remember to put it in before you have sex, and if you're having sex on the spur of the moment, you have to stop doing whatever you're doing. If you want to have sex more than once in one session, you'll need to add extra spermicide. Some girls also find that they don't like the thought of having the cap, squishy old sperm and spermicide inside them hours after bonking.

The IUD

IUD stands for *inter-uterine device* (which means thing-that-goes-in-your-womb), and is also known as *the coil.* It's a little loop of very, very thin wire on a teeny bit of plastic, and the whole caboodle gets carefully fitted into the entrance of your womb by a doctor. It works by stopping fertilised eggs from settling in your womb. Most doctors prefer not to fit an IUD for a girl who hasn't had a baby, largely because there is always a risk of infection if you have a coil, and sometimes these infections can be so bad that they ruin your chances of having a baby at all.

Advantages: It's extremely reliable (very nearly as good as the pill), you can't feel it, and it can stay in for up to five years, so you don't have to bother thinking about birth control at all.

Disadvantages: Apart from the risk of infection, there's a chance that your body could reject the coil and get rid of it. This can be painful, but it can also go unnoticed, in which case you wouldn't realise that you weren't protected any more. That's why it is always a good idea to do a little check once a week to be sure it's still there. It also makes some girls have heavy, painful periods.

The Sponge

This is a little, fat, squishy, dome-shaped thing made of soft, spongy polyurethane. Like a cap, you put it inside you, over the entrance to the womb. It's full of spermicide, which you have to activate by running the sponge under a tap and squeezing it until you can see it foaming. You put it in before you have sex (anything from 24 hours before to just a few seconds before — whenever suits you best), and leave it in for six hours afterwards. It has a loop of ribbon attached for pulling it out.

Advantages: You can buy it from chemists without a prescription, so you don't need to see a doctor, it's fairly easy to use once you get the hang of it, and neither you nor your partner can feel it. Once it's in, you can have sex more than once in one session without worrying about adding extra spermicide, and because you can put it in so far before having sex, you can relax and not worry about interrupting anything.

Disadvantages: It's not available free anywhere, and it's the most expensive method of birth control to pay for. It's also the least reliable method you can use — far less reliable than any of the others. Because you don't have any back-up from a doctor, you have to work out how to put it in yourself — and if you put it in wrong, it's obviously even less reliable. Still, if you can afford it, and you're planning to use it as back-up protection, with a condom or Femidom, it's certainly *far* better than no protection at all.

The Rhythm Method

This is when you work out in great detail exactly when

you are fertile (able to get pregnant), and then sex on those days. People who use this method work it all out either by taking their temperature every morning with a special thermometer, or by carefully studying the mucus in their vagina every day (lovely!). It's really complicated, and for there to be any chance of it actually working, you'd need a good book on the subject, at the very least. Ideally, this method should only be done with proper guidance from a medical expert.

Advantage: It's totally "natural".

Disadvantages: It's bloody complicated, time-consuming and pretty unreliable, even when you're doing it properly and don't forget, you have to stick to having sex on "safe" days.

Sterilisation

Both men and women can have operations that stop them from being able to make babies. The results are designed to be permanent, though, so most doctors would never consider performing them on a young person. After all, even if you can swear blind now that you never want kids, you might change your mind later.

Emergency Contraception

If something goes wrong with your contraception, it's not too late to do something. See page 175.

What's New?

New contraceptives are being developed all the time. This is good news, because it means more choice for everybody. Here are just some of the things that should be available in the future:

• *Contraceptive patches* — little patches you wear discreetly on your body that release hormones through your skin and into your body, a bit like those used to help you give up smoking.

• The *vaginal ring* — a small, soft, ring-shaped device that releases hormones. It would be put in place by a doctor, and keep you protected for several months at a time.

• The *progestogen IUD* — a coil that works like a normal IUD, but also releases a hormone that makes a barrier at the entrance to the womb, and stops your womb from making a lining properly every month. This means that it's even more reliable at stopping pregnancy than a normal coil, and it would also make your periods much lighter.

• A different pill — several types of new pill, using less hormones than the types available at the moment, are being tested.

• The *male pill* — scientists have been working for years to try and develop a hormone pill for boys and men. It's currently at the stage where a prototype is being tested by humans, and it's looking quite successful so far.

Sadly, there's no perfect method of birth control - they all have their drawbacks. All you can do is weigh-up the choices and go for what suits *you* best. You can always try one method and ditch it for another if you don't like it. Your GP or a doctor at your nearest Family Planning Clinic, will be able to tell you more about birth control and supply you with what you need.

CONTRACEPTION, THE LAW AND YOUR PARENTS

You probably know that the age of consent in Britain, Northern Ireland and the Republic of Ireland is 16, 17 and 18, respectively. In other words, it's against the law for a girl under that age to have sex. If you live in the Republic of Ireland, and you're under 18, you'll need to get a prescription from a doctor or clinic to buy any kind of contraception — including condoms. If you live in Great Britain or Northern Ireland, you can buy condoms, Femidoms and the sponge at any age. However, you should also be able to get free condoms, and free prescriptions for other methods of contraception if you're under age. If you were to go to your doctor or to a clinic with one of your parents, you would have no trouble at all getting fixed up with whatever you needed. If you didn't want to involve your parents, you should still be able to get contraception. If you explain clearly why you don't want your parents involved and can make it clear that you understand the advice the doctor gives you, he or she will usually go ahead and sort you out anyway, as long they feel that it's in your best interest.

But will the doctor tell my parents?
A law was passed not long ago to stop doctors doing this, but some doctors still ignore it. Hopefully yours won't, but if you're really worried, you'd be better off going to a Family Planning Clinic, or just buying condoms and waiting until you're the legal age before seeing your doctor.

Can a doctor report me to the police for having under age sex?
It's enormously unlikely. Doctors are more concerned about your health than about whether you're breaking the law. The laws about under age sex are quite complicated anyway, and it wouldn't be the girl who got in trouble with the police, but the boy she was having sex with (see Chapter Eight for lots more details). In a very extreme, serious case — say, a ten-year-old girl who was having sex with someone much older, and seemed confused and unhappy — a doctor would usually alert a social worker or the girl's parents or guardians, not the police.

YOU KNOW HOW TO PROTECT YOURSELF. BUT WILL YOU DO IT?

The chances are that you already knew some of this stuff, if not all of it. You might even feel thoroughly fed up with having endless warnings and scary information shoved down your throat. But here's a weird fact: it's not just ignorant people who put themselves at risk. You'd be amazed at how many smart, savvy, clued-up teenagers understand all the dangers... And still go right ahead and have sex without protecting themselves against pregnancy or disease.

Adults will tell you that if you think you're mature enough to have sex, then you should be mature enough to protect yourself and your sexual partners, not just sometimes, but *every time* you have sex. They'll say that if you think contraception and safe-sex take the fun out of sex, you're not mature enough to have sex. They'll tell you that if you think nothing's going to happen to *you*, because you're lucky, or because you're "careful", you're not mature enough to have sex. And they'll tell you that if you don't agree with what they say, you're not mature enough to have sex. To an extent, they're wrong. You see, they're not really talking about maturity, they're talking about having what's called a *sense of self-preservation*. When you have an in-built sense of self-preservation, you feel scared stiff at the slightest hint of danger. You feel a strong urge to protect yourself at all costs. You're not bothered by the prospect of missing out on some fun if the alternative is putting your life on the line. And instead of having a feeling, deep-down, that nothing bad is going to happen to you, you have a sneaking suspicion that if anything bad *can* happen, it probably will. This way of thinking usually comes with age — although some people never develop it at all. What's for sure, though, is that most people start having sex *long* before they start thinking this way. That's why so many people take risks.

So where does all this leave you? You can know everything there is to know and agree that it all makes perfect sense. Then the big moment comes and somehow it all seems strangely irrelevant and totally slips from your mind. There's no doubt about it, taking care of yourself is hard work when it doesn't come naturally to you. You could try and turn safe-sex into a habit — like brushing your teeth. If you force yourself to think about protection enough times, it should begin to come more naturally. Maybe another answer is to worry more. If scary thoughts about pregnancy and AIDS pop into your head, don't push them away and try to think about something else — dwell on them. Use your imagination. Scare yourself. It could save your life.

Chapter Six

SEX: EVERYTHING YOU EVER WANTED TO KNOW...

This chapter is all about the physical side of things: exactly what goes on behind closed doors, or — as the case may be — in cars, behind the bike sheds and anywhere else people get down to their personal business.

Hopefully, this chapter will help you know more about what to expect from sex. But don't forget that however well informed you are, sex is all about learning as you go. After all, you could read a hundred books about riding a bicycle, but it wouldn't really teach you how to get your balance — you wouldn't find out about that until you were actually on the seat!

This chapter won't turn you into some kind of sex expert, but it's still handy. Why? Because the better informed you are, the less scared you'll be in a sexual situation, and the less scared you are, the more you'll enjoy the whole experience.

Here are the answers to all the questions you could want to ask...

How do you French kiss?
A fair definition of a French kiss (also known as a *tongue-kiss*, a *tongue sarnie*, a *Frenchie*, a *snog* or *snogging*) would be a kiss between two people who have their mouths open. Technically speaking, a proper French kiss would also involve tongues, and go on for longer than two seconds. It doesn't sound too difficult in principal, but people tend to get very, very nervous about not doing it right, especially if they've never done it before, or if they've only ever had snogs they didn't enjoy. The good news is that once you've got the hang of the basics, which shouldn't be too difficult, there's no "right" way to French kiss, so you don't need to worry about doing it wrong. There are a few things to avoid, though. Here are the guidelines:

• No matter how you kiss, you'll get many, many extra points just for having a mouth that smells and tastes nice and lips that feel soft. Brushing your teeth and using lip balm regularly is the key. It also helps to avoid smoking or eating things like cheese and onion crisps or garlic before a snog.

• If you're chewing gum, remove it before you snog. Some people may not mind it there, but many would, and asking someone if they mind you leaving it in is just crass.

• Part your lips. Relax them totally and all the muscles around your mouth, too. Your mouth should be open just a little bit at first

• Gently press your lips against your partner's. Don't get hung up worrying about your angle of approach: most faces fit together surprisingly well and noses and other bits rarely get in the way. If you're still nervous about this, you might want to try taking your kissing-partners' face in your hands gently so that you can keep it still while you approach, or help guide it towards you.

• If one or both of you wears glasses or a dental brace, you might want to take this stage a bit more slowly and carefully to avoid unsexy clashing accidents!

• Never approach someone too forcefully — a head-butt is a bit of a turn-off. Don't approach with your mouth wide open like you were going to the dentist, either. It looks unattractive, off-putting and downright scary!

• Once your lips have met, you can get down to business. This should involve a combination of a kissing motion, and tongue-contact.

• The kissing motion ideally involves brushing your lips together, squashing them together firmly, and opening and closing your mouth slightly like you're tasting the other person's lips. It shouldn't involve mashing your lips so hard against the other person's that they can't breathe, and nor should your mouth ever end up too far open (it's not a competition to see how much of their mouth you can fit in yours).

• Tongue contact should be tentative at first, then just

about anything goes. Just be sure to keep your tongue soft and bendy, not hard and pointy. Also, avoid excessive slobbering, swirling it round and round like a washing machine, or shoving it so far into your partner's mouth that they feel sick or suffocated.

• Relax, enjoy it, and do whatever comes naturally. If you feel like closing your eyes, feel free, if you don't, don't.

• Don't worry about skill — always remember that if someone fancies you, they'll enjoy kissing you no matter how you're doing it.

• Once you feel confident, be inventive! Delicately biting your partner's lip can be very sexy. Alternating between snogging and kissing your partner's neck is usually a popular move. Use your imagination and do whatever feels nice.

• Always pay close attention to how someone is reacting. If you're not sure that your partner is enjoying the kiss or some aspect of it (too much tongue, maybe?), lighten up a bit and see what they do. If they are definitely trying to close their mouth or finish the kiss, back off right away!

• If you've never kissed anyone before, and you're mega-nervous, it can help to have a little practise on the back of your hand!

What's a love bite?

Despite its name, a love bite isn't really a bite. It's more of a very firm suck, but it leaves a kind of teeth/lip-shaped bruise that looks a bit like a bite mark, hence the name. You usually give or get love bites on the neck, and the technique is *gently* to get a little portion of your partner's flesh between your teeth, then clamp your lips down to form a vacuum and suck like crazy. Lots of people use their tongue to do some licky movements at the same time.

The funny thing about love bites is that most people agree that they don't feel terribly nice at the time. So why do people give them? It's probably because they leave a very obvious mark that lasts for several days. That's nice for the person who has given the love bite, because it can feel a bit like you've "branded" this person as your property. You also know that every time they see the mark in a mirror, or someone mentions it, they'll think of you. It's also quite nice for the person on the receiving end because displaying the mark is a bit like wearing a sign that says: "Hello! I've been having a passionate session with someone and I'm a bit of a saucepot, am I not?" or "Look! Someone fancies me!" Some people actually enjoy the way a love bite *feels*, although the majority find that just being lightly nibbled, bitten, or sucked feels a lot nicer and more exciting than the rather violent love bite, which is not unlike getting stuck to an industrial-strength Hoover with teeth.

On a dead serious note, it's essential, for safety reasons, to avoid giving love bites on the central-front area of the neck, where the jugular vein is. If you're biting a boy, you'd want to avoid that area anyway, because the Adam's apple — the little bumpy bit in the middle — is very sensitive. When choosing a good site for a love bite, it's thoughtful to go for an area that can be hidden under a collar or hair — after all, you don't want your partner to get embarrassed or into trouble. Giving someone a love bite on the cheek has got to be one of the most irritating things you could possibly do. Also, avoid bony bits like shoulders because it's hard to get a mouthful of flesh without hurting your partner. The most important love bite rule is *never* to bite hard: quite apart from the fact that it could be dangerous, it bloody well hurts.

What's heavy petting?

This is a rather old-fashioned word which describes the large selection of activities that can go on during a passionate snogging session. It can also be known as *getting off* with someone, and in America (and therefore probably in most of the films you've seen) it's called *making out*. All these words can refer to something that's fairly innocent, and also to something far more heavy. They cover just about anything from general cuddling and rubbing up and down against each other, to fondling and groping someone's bosoms, bottom or crotch through their clothes, to steamy touchings underneath clothes, or with the clothes undone or removed. It can also mean much more intimate stuff, like kissing, licking or sucking someone's nipples or putting fingers inside a girl's fanny, or up someone's bottom. It can even mean masturbating your partner: i.e. playing with their willy or clitoris in a way that's designed to make them have an orgasm. Phew!

Many teenagers find that for a while they enjoy petting even more than sex, because they feel more relaxed with the idea. It all seems less of a big deal — there's no pressure and you don't have to worry about protection. It's also exciting and passionate — all in all, a very nice experience indeed, and one which proves that you don't have to have full sex to have fun.

So can you have an orgasm just from heavy petting?
Oh yes. In fact, a girl is more likely to come during petting than sex, as her clitoris is likely to get the kind of attention that causes orgasms. For both partners, all that rubbing, groping and general excitement is often a strong enough combination to make them come. If you're masturbating each other, it's even more likely.

Do a lot of people do that?
Sure, if they feel comfortable enough together. Masturbating a boy is commonly called a *hand-job*. You might also hear it called *wanking* or *wanking off*, just like regular masturbation. There's no particular word for masturbating a girl, but some people call it *diddling*, *playing with*, *fingering* or the ever-popular *wanking off*.

How do you do it?
Generally speaking, the idea is to touch and move your partner's sensitive bits exactly the same way they would if they were playing with themselves. Unfortunately, you're unlikely to have the faintest clue of how that's done. You can check back to chapter two to remind yourself of the basics. Here are some more pointers:

How to make a boy feel wonderful (and hopefully have an orgasm)

• Firmly grip the willy just below the "head" (see page 3 for a diagram), then start rhythmically moving your hand up and down the shaft, right from the base to the top. If you're gripping firmly enough, you should find that your hand slides easily up and down without ever losing contact, because the foreskin is in between your hand and the willy, and that's how it's designed to move. It doesn't make any difference if the boy is circumcised or not.

• If the boy looks like he's happy with this, you can start moving your hand faster, and make the up and down movement a bit shorter, concentrating on moving over just the top half of the willy, especially the bit where the shaft meets the head, which feels especially nice.

• It's important to try and maintain the same speed and rhythm throughout, and keep your grip firm — not too tight, but not too delicate either.

• If your partner moves your hand into a new position, or says "Faster!", don't feel insulted — he's not criticising you, just making things easier for you by letting you know what he likes.

• Lots of boys really like having their balls "cupped" or stroked while all this is going on — but be gentle — they're very delicate and sensitive!

• You'll know for sure when the boy has come, because semen will spurt out of the top of his willy and he'll probably make some kind of noise or exclamation! Don't stop the movement or take your hand away until the spurting is finished.

• Some boys come very quickly (it could be as quick as a few seconds, especially if he was very excited to start with), others take longer.

• It's polite to avoid going "Eeeeew! yuk" and staring in disgust at your hands, clothes, or anything else that the spunk has ended up on!

• If you've been at it for ages and ages without your partner coming, and your arm feels like it's going to drop off, it's best to rest for a bit. If you really want to give up, do. You could even suggest that he finishes off the job for you — this means he ends up happy, not frustrated, and you get the golden opportunity to see an expert at work and learn from it — after all boys know their willies better than anyone else!

• There are other methods of making a boy feel nice or have an orgasm. Many boys like to put their willy under their partner's armpit and move it in and out – it sounds funny, but it works! Also, if a girl has largish bosoms, she can hold them together to form a snug place for a willy to slide in and out between. This is most easily done if the boy is sitting on top of the girl, so if the boy is loads heavier than the girl, it's best avoided!

How to make a girl feel wonderful (and hopefully have an orgasm)

• Many boys think that girls masturbate by sticking willy-shaped objects in themselves, and therefore to play with a girl, you have to use your finger like a willy. If you read Chapter Two, you'll know this isn't the case. Having said that, some girls do thoroughly enjoy their partner sliding his fingers quickly in and out of her, like a willy (this is sometimes rather crudely called *finger-fucking*), but most girls are unlikely to actually have an orgasm like that.

• A girl feels most sexual pleasure in her clitoris, so that's the bit to concentrate on. Whereas the willy isn't hard to find (unless you're really short-sighted), the girl's clitoris is a slightly trickier customer. Taking a good look at the diagram in Chapter One should help, but if you're in the height of passion, you're not going to want to say, "Hang on a sec whilst I have a really close look at your privates". You'll actually need to find it by touch. Here's how: gently put your hand between your partner's legs and try to find the warm, damp area where the lips of her vagina meet. Lightly push one of your fingers in a tiny bit (you're not trying to get inside her vagina, just between the lips) and slide it slowly upwards until you feel that the gap has stopped. Here, or a tiny bit higher up, you should feel a tiny bobble. This is it!

• When you touch the clitoris, make sure you're touching the little bit of skin that covers it, or the whole area around it, not the actual clitoris (which is very sensitive). Try doing it with one or two fingers, pressing it with very light pressure, making tiny movements either up and down, or round and round, keeping up a steady rhythm. You could also stroke or rub the whole area with the palm of your hand or your fingers. Never be too rough.

• If you've got the right place and movement, your partner should be enjoying it lots. If not, she might helpfully replace your hand in a slightly different spot. Don't feel insulted — she's just helping you get to know her better!

• If your fingers are a bit damp, it can help make your movements smoother. You can use the girl's natural lubrication, or just lick your fingers.

• It's essential to understand that girls' orgasms are very different to boys'. A boy would probably come from being wanked off even if he was in a very unsexy situation, because it's largely a physical reaction. A girl, however, might not be able to come even if she wanted to, for a number of reasons, including being embarrassed, nervous, pressured or distracted.

• Because girls don't spurt anything out when they come, and because they don't usually thrash around and shriek like women do in movies, it could be hard to tell when your partner has come. If you're lucky, she might make a noise or gasp, or she might shudder or go tense for a brief moment. She may also move your hand away, because once a girl has come, her clitoris usually feels too sensitive to be touched for a while. If you're still in doubt, ask!

• If you've been at it for ages, and it doesn't seem like your partner is going to come, don't feel too bad. Remember that you can enjoy petting (and sex) without having an orgasm.

• It's best not to suggest to a girl that she "finish herself off" — very few girls feel comfortable about masturbating in front of someone else.

• Interestingly enough, some girls can also come from having other parts of their bodies touched in the right way. A girl with super-sensitive bosoms can have an orgasm without her partner even touching her clitoris, if he or she strokes, caresses, licks or sucks her boobs. It's also not unheard of for girls to be able to come from having their backs or tummies stroked or their hair touched and played with!

• Unlike boys, girls can come many times in one petting or sex session. Although the clitoris feels sensitive right after an orgasm, it usually feels fine again quite soon, and you'll find that if you carry on playing with your partner, she'll be able to come again, if you both want to try.

• The official record for the most orgasms in one session is 50! It's held by an American woman who was helping sex-researchers with a study of women's orgasms at the time. She claimed afterwards that she thought she could have managed a few more! This is obviously rather extreme, but it just goes to illustrate how different girls are to boys in this way — whilst the average bloke can only manage about four orgasms in one sex session (and it's likely to be less), the average girl can just keep on going!

The above descriptions may sound a bit clinical and yukky. That's because they don't mention all the little things that make petting loving and passionate instead of technical. Kissing, saying nice things, stroking your partner's hair or body, cuddling, pressing your body up against theirs, and showing or telling them how much you're enjoying yourself is what makes the difference.

Does it matter if you don't have an orgasm when you're

petting? Someone told me that it was dangerous...
You might have heard about something that boys can get, called *blue balls.* When a boy gets very sexually excited, blood rushes into his willy (giving him an erection) and also his balls, making them feel firmer and fuller, right? When he has an orgasm, all that blood rushes away again. If he doesn't have one, the blood goes away and everything goes back to normal eventually, but it takes much longer. Until that happens, a boy can sometimes have an uncomfortable, tight, achy feeling in his balls, and they can also look slightly blue (because of all those full blood vessels). This can be a bit scary, and a bit annoying, but it's not at all dangerous. Some boys try to use blue balls as an excuse to put pressure on their girlfriends to have sex immediately, saying that if they don't do it, they'll be in terrible pain or suffer terrible damage. This just isn't true, so boys: don't say it, and girls: don't believe a word of it!

Can girls get blue balls too?
Obviously girls don't have balls, but yes, experts have recently discovered that there is a similar thing that girls can get if they get very, very aroused without coming. Again, it's a swollen, achy feeling in the privates (and sometimes a mild, low tummy-ache), but although it's annoying, it can't do you any damage.

Is foreplay the same as heavy petting?

Pretty much. The difference is that foreplay means you're leading up to having full, penetrative sex, while petting is done just for the fun of it, without leading up to anything else. The other difference is that in foreplay, you'd probably want to avoid the boy coming, in case he didn't manage to get hard again for sex.

Do you have to have foreplay before you have sex?
No, but it helps to get you both relaxed and in the mood, so it's a nice idea. Foreplay is especially useful for girls, because it can help get them excited enough to make the natural wetness which helps make sex more comfortable.

Can you get pregnant from heavy petting or foreplay?
It depends. You only need a teeny little bit of semen to find its way into a girl's fanny for her to get pregnant, and, believe it or not, it *is* possible for this to happen accidentally during petting or foreplay. If a boy comes *near* a girl's privates, some of the semen *could* find its way inside her — amazing but true. If either of you get semen on your hands, it could also end up just where you don't want it. It's safe to say that if a girl's got her knickers on, she's pretty unlikely to get pregnant, but remember that knickers are not considered a reliable form of contraception! To be safe, always be fully aware of where semen goes.

What about catching diseases?

Boys aren't really at risk from petting or foreplay. Girls have a bigger risk if there's semen about. If you've both got your undies on, or the boy doesn't come at all, we're talking about pretty safe sex. However, if oral sex is part of your petting or foreplay, you've got all the risks that come with it. Flick back to Chapter Five for a reminder about what's risky and what's not, AIDS-wise. You'll find info about other diseases and how you can catch them in Chapter Eight.

What's oral sex?

Oral means "to do with the mouth" and oral sex is the general term for doing things to your partner's privates with your mouth. When you have oral sex with a boy, it's called *fellatio*, but you're more likely to have heard it called a *blow-job*, *giving head*, *sucking off* or *going down* on someone. The proper word for oral sex with a girl is *cunnilingus*, but again, few people actually use it — most people talk about *going down* on someone or *eating out*, or use terms like *muff-diving* or *eating pussy*.

Oral sex isn't "pervy" — it's a very normal, natural and nice part of sex. Still, a lot of people of both sexes don't like doing it to other people, and quite a few girls and some boys (but not many!) don't particularly enjoy having it done to them. This can be because they don't like the way it feels, but more often it's because they feel self-conscious about someone's head being that close to their privates — the worry and embarrassment that their bits might look or smell funny stops them from being able to relax and enjoy it. As with any other activity, you should always be thoughtful about what your partner does and doesn't want to do.

How do you do it?

The general idea of oral sex is to lick, kiss and suck your partner's sensitive bits. This feels very nice for the person on the receiving end (unless, they don't happen to feel comfortable about it). For the person doing the work, it's quite tiring, and it must be said that most of the pleasure comes from knowing your partner is enjoying it.

If you've ever tried to write, open a door or turn on the telly using just your mouth and tongue, you'll be well aware of just how much easier it is to do things with your hands. Because of this simple fact, oral sex is usually not as easy to master as some other sexual things. Practise certainly helps, although being "good" at performing oral sex isn't really all that important. Just the fact that you're prepared to stick your face in someone's nether regions is quite a nice gesture in itself, and your partner should be happy and grateful that you're making the effort to give them pleasure, rather than giving you marks out of ten. If you discover that's not the case with your partner, then you're with the wrong person.

If you still feel you'd like some more specific info about it, read on:

Giving a boy a blow job

• The first thing to know about a blow-job (and possibly most important), is not to blow! Blowing on the willy like as if it was hot soup won't do anything at all, and actually blowing down the tip of the willy, or blowing while it's in your mouth, can be incredibly dangerous because you risk sending an air bubble into your boyfriend's internal organs. Yes, the name is misleading. Stupid, isn't it?

• What you actually do is open your mouth and lower your head onto your partner's willy, guiding it with your hands, until it's an inch or so inside your mouth. If you feel like you're choking, gagging or retching, it's probably in too far!

• Close your mouth around the tip of the willy, being sure to protect it from your teeth either by keeping them well parted, or curling your lips over them. Start sucking to create a vacuum pressure inside your mouth around the willy. You can get an idea of what that feels like by sucking your thumb hard with your mouth closed.

• Now the idea is to grip the base of the willy and move your head up and down, still sucking all the time, so that the willy is slipping in and out between your lips.

• When you've got a comfortable rhythm going, you could try flicking your tongue around the tip of the willy at the same time.

• Some people also move their willy-gripping hand up and down in time with their mouth.

• Some people also like to stop occasionally to lick the tip of the willy and the bit where the head meets the shaft (see diagram on page 3) with fast, flicking tongue movements, or lick up and down the whole length of the willy, before taking the willy in their mouth again and carrying on.

• Many boys like to have their balls licked, kissed and gently sucked too (but never forget how delicate and sensitive they are).

• Some boys enjoy having their bum-hole stimulated too, so it might be worth a try while you're down that way! Obviously, you'd have to like someone a heck of a lot to want to lick their bum — using your finger is a bit less daunting!

• Ideally, it's polite for the boy to let you know when he's about to come, so that you could finish the job with your hand if you really didn't want him to come in your mouth. There's nothing wrong with someone coming in your mouth, but if you're not expecting it and it's never happened to you before, it can be a bit of a shock — and it would be nice of your partner to realise that.

• Some people think semen tastes disgusting, some

don't mind the taste, and others rather like it. However, even those who rather like it would agree that it doesn't taste delicious exactly — it's kind of salty. Those who don't, often say that it's the texture they find funny as much as the taste — it can be surprisingly thick.

• If someone comes in your mouth, you don't have to swallow it. Many boys take it as a big compliment if you do, and a bit of an insult if you don't, but don't let this worry you too much. Making the effort to swallow can be a loving gesture, but if it's going to end up with you retching and turning a delicate shade of green, then it detracts somewhat from the original sentiment, and probably isn't worth bothering.

• Spitting semen out is perfectly acceptable and polite as long as you do it discreetly and nicely. Gracefully and quietly spitting it into your hand, like you would with an olive pip, is fine. Violently expelling it several feet with a loud "Pah!" isn't so good. Nor is holding it in your mouth with an alarmed look of repulsion on your face and making pained noises while you frantically search for a tissue.

Going down on a girl

• Remember the clitoris? That's your main target again, only this time you're using your mouth and tongue instead of your hands.

• There are a few different techniques. For instance you

can make repeated, rhythmic kissing and sucking motions, you can lick slowly and you can flick your tongue in quick, sharp, lapping motions. You can also suck and flick your tongue at the same time. Why not try everything, and see what your partner likes best?

• Always mind your teeth!

• If your partner seems uncomfy and jumpy, you might be touching her clitoris directly, which feels very sensitive — try to avoid doing that.

• You don't have to just concentrate on the clitoris — licking and kissing all around that area feels nice.

• Lots of girls find that oral sex makes them have an orgasm quite quickly. Others find it takes longer, and many more rarely come during oral sex at all. The best thing to do, until you know what the score is with your partner, is to carry on for as long as she's enjoying it and you're not getting too knackered! If she doesn't seem to be enjoying it, or she seems to be getting tired of it, move on to doing something else.

Can you get pregnant or catch a disease by having oral sex?
A girl can't get pregnant by having oral sex, even if she swallows a boy's semen. However there is a certain amount of risk regarding AIDS and other STDs (see Chapters Five and Eight).

So what about the real thing?
Call it what you will — *sexual intercourse, penetration, copulation, coitus, making-love, bonking, shagging, fucking, screwing, humping, shafting, poking, rumping, rodgering, going all-the-way* — penetrative sex is seen as the big deal to end all big deals in the world of sexual encounters. This is quite odd, considering that oral sex, playing with one another and even general petting are pretty intense, intimate experiences, too. If you've done any of those things, then you've experienced quite a lot of what sex is about, and may not find penetration to be the huge leap into the unknown that you'd expected.

Right. Let's say that me and my partner have a snog or foreplay or whatever, and we're going to go all the way.

What happens next?
No two love-making sessions are ever identical, but here are a few basic things you can expect.
• At some point you'll remove some or all of your clothes — your pants at the very least, or it might be a bit tricky!

• When the boy's willy is hard, you'll put on a condom (unless you're mad, or you've got an extremely good reason not to).

• Once you're in a comfortable position, it's time for the boy to slip his willy into the girl. The boy can take charge of this bit, but it's *tons* easier if you do it together. The girl can help by either guiding the willy with her hand, or just wriggling herself into the right position.

• Once the willy is comfortably inside, the boy moves his hips so that it thrusts in and out. The boy will probably set the pace, because he's moving his willy in a way that excites him. It is possible for a couple to have sex without the girl budging an inch, but it's extremely boring for the girl, and quite boring for the boy too. The girl should move too, in time with her partner, although these movements don't always come as easily and naturally to girls as they do to boys.

• There's no doubt that a girl's body isn't quite as well designed for sex as a boy's. Although most girls like the feeling of having a boy's willy inside them, they don't actually get that much in the way of amazing physical sensations from what's going on inside. For girls, the nice feelings come from the whole area around the vagina — yes, we're talking about the clitoris again. Lots of girls find that just the in-and-out motion moves all their parts in a way that feels nice, but others find they need to actually press their clitoris against the boy to get that exciting feeling. Meanwhile, a lot more girls find it ruddy difficult to work out exactly what they need to do. Many girls solve this problem by touching their clitorises, or having their partner do it for them, while they're making love. This is easier in some positions than others (see further down).

• It's pretty rare for a boy not to come during sex, as

long as he is relaxed and happy. However it's remarkably common for a girl not to, especially if she hasn't had sex many times, because she's not yet familiar with what she needs to do. It's simply not as easy for girls to have orgasms during penetration as it is for boys, but most girls eventually find a particular position, movement or other trick that makes the difference. Sex experts at the London Institute of Human Sexuality say that in surveys of young women in their teens and twenties, half don't have orgasms at all, and more than half don't have them through penatrative sex. The good news is that the older a woman gets, the more likely she is to be able to come during sex. But remember: as wonderful as orgasms can be, they're really not the be-all and end-all: you *can* enjoy sex without having one.

What's the best position to have sex in?

There are lots of different positions you can have sex in, and which is the best is a matter of personal taste. Mind you, you don't have to pick just one — you can change over as many times as you like! These are the best-known, most popular positions:

- *Boy on top* — the girl lies down, or sits and leans back, with her legs apart.
  Advantages: You can kiss, and see each other's faces. The boy can move freely.
  Disadvantages: The girl can't move that freely.
- *Girl on top* — the boy lies down, but with his knees a

bit bent so that he can still move his hips freely. His partner either lies or half-sits on top, with her knees on either side of him.

Advantages: You can kiss, and see each other's faces. The girl can move freely, and is more likely to have an orgasm, because she can control the movements. If the girl sits up, her partner can touch her bosoms and clitoris.

Disadvantages: The boy can't move that freely. Some girls feel shy about being "in charge".

- *From-behind* — this position is sometimes called *doggie-style*. The girl kneels on all fours with her partner behind her. You can also do it so that the girl is lying on her front with her partner on top of her. This position *doesn't* mean that the boy's willy is up the girl's bum (although if you *were* having anal sex, this would probably be the position you'd use).

Advantages: Both partners can move freely. The boy can touch the girl's bosoms and clitoris. The willy fits more snugly in this position, so it's often a favourite of boys who worry a lot about having a small willy. Boys who like looking at their partner's bum get a nice treat!

Disadvantages: You can't kiss or see each other's faces. If the boy has a very long willy, it might go in too deep in this position and hurt the girl.

- *Side by side* — the boy and girl lie on their sides, either facing each other, or with the boy behind the girl.

Advantages: Both partners can move freely. You both have at least one arm free to cuddle and touch each other. You can kiss and see each other (if you're doing it face-to-face). Not too tiring.

Disadvantages: Can be tricky to get the willy in at first.

• *Sitting down* — this is usually done with the girl sitting on the boy's lap.

Advantages: You can kiss and see each other's faces. Both of your have your arms free, so you can cuddle and touch each other lots.

Disadvantages: Can be tiring for the boy, and he can't move his hips that freely.

• *Standing up* — unless you've got great balance, you need a wall as support for this position.

Advantages: You can kiss and see each other's faces. Both of you have your arms free for touching and cuddling. You can use this position in exciting places like showers and cupboards!

Disadvantages: Can be tiring for both partners and dead tricky (or impossible) if there's a big height-difference.

There are other positions, but most of them are just variations on these basic ones — i.e. boy on top, with the girls legs in the air, so her knees are by her head and her feet are resting on her partner's shoulders. Other alternative positions can be dictated by where you are. For instance, if you were in a car, the girl might sit on the back seat with her legs apart, and her partner could sort of kneel up in front of her. If you were in a kitchen, the girl might sit on a low counter and wrap her legs round her partner as he stands facing her.

Someone told me that there was a famous book that showed you thousands of sexual positions, including some really weird ones...
You might be thinking of an old, mystic, eastern book called *The Kama Sutra*. It's full of odd drawings of positions that look either physically impossible or jolly uncomfortable and probably not much fun (unless your idea of fun is slipping a disc in your back or falling off the bed and concussing yourself).

What's anal sex?
Anal is a word that means "to do with your bum", so no prizes for guessing that anal sex is when a boy puts his willy into somone's bottom hole (the proper term is *rectum*). It's also sometimes known as *buggery*, or *buggering* someone.

Anal sex usually feels rather nice for the owner of the willy, but the owner of the bottom may not find it so pleasant. Most people find that it hurts rather a lot, which puts them off trying it a second time. Others just don't like the feeling, because it reminds them of needing to poo, which isn't terribly sexy at all. Still, many people find they like it, and do it regularly, despite the risks — and it certainly has more than its fair share of risks... Firstly, it's a big AIDS risk (as was explained in the last chapter) and you're at risk from sexually transmitted diseases too (see Chapter Eight). Secondly, you're still at risk even if you use a condom, because many condoms aren't tough enough to withstand the pressure of anal sex, and can tear while you're at it. However, you can buy extra-strong condoms especially for anal sex. Thirdly, there's also a danger of infection from bottomy germs, so a willy or finger which has been up a bum should never go near a vagina or mouth afterwards without being thoroughly washed. People who are regularly on the receiving end of anal sex, over a long period of time, also risk weakening and stretching their sphincter muscle — the muscle around the opening of their bum. This can mean that you lose a lot of your natural control over farting and even pooing. It might sound funny, but you'd be unlikely to find it at all hilarious if it happened to you. Finally, if you turn to the section on sex and the law in Chapter Eight, you'll also find that anal sex is illegal — although most people ignore this.

Can you get pregnant from anal sex?
Technically, no. But you've got to remember that a girl's bottom-hole is not very far from her vagina at all, so escaped semen wouldn't have to make a very long journey to get into it. If that happened, she could indeed get pregnant.

Do boys who are gay always have anal sex?
No. Two boys together will usually do the same things

that a boy and a girl do together — kissing, cuddling, petting, playing with each other and having oral sex. Sometimes — but not always — they also decide to have anal sex.

How do two girls have sex?
Many people imagine that lesbian sex involves one girl pretending to be a man, and even wearing a pretend willy. This is crap. Girls who are gay want to have sex with other girls because they like girls, and girls' bodies — therefore they're not at all bothered that there's no willy involved. Apart from penetration, lesbians do the same things that heterosexuals do — kissing, cuddling, petting, playing with each other, having oral sex. Sometimes two girls might also decide to lie one on top of the other and rub their groins together, and they might also put their fingers inside one another. However, they would do both of these things simply because it feels nice — not because they want to pretend that one of them is a boy.

How do you have sex if you've got a physical disability?
Any limitations and difficulties you might have depends very much on your particular disability. Generally speaking, though, people who are physically challenged can (and do) have sex just the same as everyone else. The biggest annoyance you're likely to face is able-bodied people who can't see that you're a sexual person just like them.

On the practical side, it helps to know very clearly what you want and need your partner to do, and not shy away from explaining it to them. For instance, if you use a wheelchair, you might want some help from your partner to get you out of the chair and into a comfortable position. If you're paralysed, then it's also important for your partner to understand your body. Many people who are paralysed from the waist down find that their sexual organs react physically to being touched just like anyone else's — a boy's willy can get hard, a girl's fanny can get wet — even if they can't feel anything. It would be essential for your partner to know this. If they didn't they might assume that whatever they were doing felt lovely for you, when in fact, you're bored stiff and wishing they would touch the parts of you that you can feel. Similarly, if you have a condition like Cerebral Palsy, where you can feel everything but have limited control over your movements, it would be dead important for your partner to understand the condition before you had sex.

The more your partner understands you, the better and more relaxed sex will be for you both.

Talking doesn't have to be limited to telling your partner what you need: it's equally important that they understand what you don't need. If you're deaf or blind, for instance, you're unlikely to need much help at all, and it can be very, very annoying to have someone giving you special treatment when you don't need or want it.

If you have a disability, or you're involved with someone who has, you might want to check out some of the extremely helpful leaflets and booklets which are available from special organisations. Details are in the back of this book.

People in films always make lots of odd noises during sex. Do you have to do that?
People in films seem to think you have to, but you don't really! You should just do whatever comes naturally. Some people don't feel the urge to make much noise at all, others find they make all sorts of noises without even realising it — everything from gentle panting (because they're breathless from moving around a lot or just sheer excitement) to gasps, grunts, groans, moans and even shrieks and yells (usually because they're enjoying themselves so much). Generally, though, people don't make half as much noise in real life as they do in films!

Should I make noises even if I don't feel like it?
It's usually better to act naturally — silly fake moans and yelps are pretty pointless and can be quite irritating. On the other hand, if you're totally silent, you partner might worry that you're bored rigid and having a horrible time, so making the odd noise can be a nice gesture. If you're making noises deliberately, though, always err on the side of subtlety. A slightly panty quickening of your breathing will let your partner know you're happy, and isn't embarrassing to do. Suddenly letting rip with a fake noise — especially if you're

usually quiet — could make your partner think you've suddenly got leg cramp or something.

Is it okay to talk during sex?

Again, being natural is always the best thing. If you feel like saying something, say it (as long as it's to do with sex — suddenly announcing that you don't fancy Arsenal's chances in the next F.A. Cup probably won't go down too well). Appreciative comments are always nice, because they make your partner feel confident and good. Some can also help let your partner know what you like (for instance — "I love it when you do that"), so all in all, talking during sex is great, if you feel like it.

Whatever you say, think before you say it, and avoid comments you've heard in films or books, especially if you don't feel 100 per cent comfortable saying them. Things like "Oooh baby, that feels good", "Give it to me, big boy" or "I'm gonna make you purr like a kitten" normally sound fairly stupid. Incidentally, it's also a good idea to steer clear of saying "I love you" during sex, even if you feel like it (and if the sex is wonderful, it's not unlikely that you would!). Of course, its a lovely thing to say, but it's heavy implications could scare your partner and stress them out. Alternatively, they might be delighted, but worry later that you didn't really mean it, and only said it because you were enjoying the sex so much. "I love you" is always best said at some other time.

What's talking dirty?
This is when you pay a compliment, talk about what you're doing or reveal something else you'd like to do, using more rude words than normal. Lots of people find talking dirty an incredible turn-on, whether they're talking or listening. Others find it scary, threatening or off-putting, so if you're planning to try, start gently and check your partner's reaction before going any further.

What happens if I accidentally do something embarrassing during sex? I think I'd die!
Most adults can tell you at least one embarrassing thing that's happened to them during sex, from farting or burping to getting hiccups or a fit of the giggles. It's reassuring to know that those things happen to everybody — although you'd never know it from watching movies and TV, reading raunchy books or even hearing people talking about sex, would you? Sex in real life is not all unbridled passions and soft lighting. It's also messy, funny and sometimes a bit silly. Even if you can fight the occasional natural urge to fart or burp, your body can make all sorts of odd noises during sex. Tummies can rumble, two chests pressing together can make air escape in a very farty-sounding way, and billions of girls are horrified to find out the hard way about *fanny-farts* — a highly embarrassing parping noise that can occur when air escapes from the vagina after the boy takes his willy out. This is especially common if you've been doing it doggie-style, because more air seems to get in that way. The point is

that none of these things are a big deal unless you turn them into one. If something embarrassing happens to you, just go "oops!" or ignore it altogether, then try to get back in the right mood by reassuring yourself that it wasn't so terrible. After all, if you and your partner are close enough to have sex, you should be comfortable enough to cope with a silly little thing like this. If your partner is mature and nice, they'll either laugh along with you or ignore it, and not mention it afterwards. If they're stupid about it, or tell other people, ditch them pronto and be thankful that you discovered how immature and mean they were before you got any further into a relationship with them.

Can I have sex during my period?

If you and your partner don't mind, there's no reason not to. Lots of people feel fine about it, other don't. The only way to find out how your partner feels is to ask. If you do have sex during your period, it's smart to put down a towel first, to avoid staining the bed (sofa, floor, car, whatever).

What do you think about during sex?

If you're thoroughly enjoying the sex, then you'll be drifting away, thinking about nothing in particular. If it's your first time, or your first time with a new partner, you might be thinking more specifically about what you're doing. If you're not enjoying it that much, your mind might wander to everyday things, which can't be helped. Some people deliberately think about sexy things, or fantasise, which can add enormously to the pleasure of sex. Many — especially girls, find that fantasising can make it much easier to have an orgasm.

Is it wrong to imagine that the person you're having sex with is somebody else?
Who's to say what's right or wrong? Many, many people enjoy shutting their eyes and pretending that they're actually shagging Keanu Reeves or Naomi Campbell or whoever, whether it's a fleeting thought, or a long, elaborate fantasy. It's pretty harmless to do this now and again, as long as you don't tell your partner about it. If you do it every time you have sex, and you don't think you could possibly get excited without doing it, then perhaps you should think carefully about your true feelings for your partner, and ask yourself if you really want to be having sex with them at all.

How long does it take to have sex?
You've probably noticed by now that there's no such thing as normal, where sex is concerned. Sometimes it can last for an hour, a couple of hours or even longer. Other times it's over in a few minutes. If the boy suffers from *premature ejaculation* (coming too quickly), it could even be a matter of seconds — see Chapter Eight for more details. Between ten minutes and half an hour — including foreplay — is about average.

People often brag — or write song lyrics — about

having sex "all night long", but longer is not necessarily better. If you really did it all night long the chances are that you'd both end up knackered, achy, sore and a bit bored.

Don't bother worrying about how long sex goes on for; it's not a competition. The most important thing is that you both enjoy it.

How do you know when it's over?

In theory, sex is over when both partners have come. In reality, it's over when the boy has come, because, with all the best will in the world, he's not going to be able to carry on bonking after that. Obviously this could put a bit of pressure on the boy to make sure that his partner comes first, or at the same time. This is easier said than done, since it's difficult, if not impossible, to stop yourself from coming if you're close to it — especially when you're young. Another fact to consider is that the girl may not manage to come at all, especially if it's her first time. If both partners still felt in a sexy mood once the boy had come, they could start cuddling and kissing again, and the boy could try to give his partner an orgasm by playing with her. There's also nothing to say that you have to have sex just once in an evening — if no one's tired, and the boy can manage to get hard, you can do it all again!

What do you do after you've finished having sex?

It all depends on how you feel. Some people like to lie

cuddling for a while. Others prefer to roll apart and get their breath back. Once the willy is out, the boy is probably going to want to take the condom off and get rid of it at some point, but there's no sense in rushing about frantically when you could be enjoying what's sometimes called the *Afterglow* — the delicious warm, happy, loving and close feeling that comes from having good sex with someone you care about.

Chapter Seven

GREAT SEX

GREAT EXPECTATIONS...

Here are two typical comments from people about their first sexual experiences:

I thought that losing my virginity would be the most amazing thing that ever happened to me, but afterwards, all I could think was "Is that it? That can't be what all the fuss is about!" I didn't really enjoy it much at all. Is there something wrong with me?

I recently had sex for the first time and it was quite nice, but also a bit disappointing because it wasn't at all how I expected it to be...

No matter how much you know about sex, how well prepared you are and how lovely your partner is, you can never guarantee that sex is going to turn out perfectly. Most people find that at best, their first sexual experience isn't quite the way they thought it would be, and at worst, can't figure out for the life of them why anyone actually bothers doing it at all! This isn't because sex is actually a very useless pursuit and everyone's been fibbing about it all along. When sex is good, it can be just about the most fun two people can have together. Great sex is a magical combination of the right people doing the right things together. Sometimes — but not all that often — people find that magic comes together the very first time they do it. But more often, it doesn't, and people find that losing their virginity is just their first step towards great sex. Let's get something straight, though: even if your first experience isn't perfect, you can still enjoy it, big time. The real problem is that people often feel disappointed afterwards, because they were expecting fireworks, earth quakes, choirs of angels bursting into the Hallelujah Chorus above the bed and all that kind of malarkey. Think about it this way: two people are going skiing for the first time. One is expecting to have a wonderful adventure, skiing down a nice, gentle little slope and gradually getting confident on their skis. The other has spent ages day-dreaming about swooping through the air off towering ski-jumps at seventy miles an hour. When they finally go skiing, they both have a pretty good time, but one of them is going to be happy about it and the other is probably going to feel bitterly cheated and disappointed. You see, it's not about what actually happens, but how it compares to what you expected. Sex is the same deal, and there's only one way to make sure sex lives up to all your expectations: have very realistic expectations.

Nowadays, most people go into sex with totally the

wrong expectations. Why? Well, think about this: back in the old days, no one really had the faintest idea of what sex was all about until they actually found out for themselves. Things have changed. Most of us get a bit of sex education at school. Many of us are lucky enough to have open-minded parents, or older brothers, sisters and friends who'll answer a few of our questions. But even these handy sources rarely get down to the nitty gritty and tell us what we really want to know: *what sex is actually like*. To get some idea of what we can expect, we have to look elsewhere and the search usually ends at the cinema, video shop or sitting-room couch. Yes indeed, the place that most people get their info on what sex is like is films or dramas on telly that have sex-scenes in them. After all, this is your only chance to actually *see* things for yourself (unless you count accidentally walking into your parents' bedroom while they're at it, which is more likely to make you chuck up your dinner than say 'Hurrah! What a fabulous educational opportunity!').

Forming an impression of what sex is like by watching actors and actresses pretending to do it is not particularly helpful. At best it's a bit misleading, at worst it could end up with your early experiences of sex leaving you anxious, confused, disappointed or miserable. Sex is rarely anything like it is in the movies. That's not to say that it's not as exciting or romantic or fabulous. It's just that everyone does it differently, and you'll enjoy sex much more if you don't have any set ideas about how it "should" be. There's no greater bummer than constantly worrying that you're not making quite the same thrusty bottom movements or moany-groany noises as you saw on the screen, that you're somehow *not doing it properly*. Sex is not about doing things in any particular order or style. It's about enjoying yourself and making sure that your partner is enjoying it too. Sure, go ahead and watch actors and actresses pretending to bonk if you find it entertaining, but never confuse it with real life.

SO WHAT MAKES SEX GREAT?

Sadly, there's no magic formula for great sex — it's more complex than that. However, there's a good chance that sex will be wonderful if:

- You and your partner are relaxed and happy.

- Both of you really want to have sex and have no doubts about it.

- You both fancy each other like mad.

- You're protecting yourselves against pregnancy and diseases.

- You both feel comfy with your own bodies.

- Neither of you feel embarrassed or guilty about having sex or enjoying it.

• Neither of you feel any pressure to be "good" in bed, or "live up to" your partner's expectations.

• You really want your partner to enjoy the experience as much as you do.

• You both feel comfortable enough to laugh or shrug it off if anything goes wrong, or if anything embarrassing happens.

• You know you'll still care about each other even if the sex doesn't turn out to be that brilliant.

You might notice that most of these factors depend on your having a good relationship. This is no coincidence — the best sex happens between people who care about each other and feel comfortable together.

DO YOU HAVE TO BE IN LOVE TO HAVE GREAT SEX?

If you're actually in love, the chances of having great sex are much better than if you're not. It's true, though, that some people manage to have great sex without having a relationship at all. Usually, they just adore the experience of sex, the way that other people adore surfing or horse-riding, and they're not that bothered about the emotional side.

Sex for sex's sake *can* be wonderful between two

people who think the same way. However it can be hard for someone who wants to shag just for fun, no strings attached, to find a like-minded partner. Most people want some kind of relationship, and have sex for deeper, more emotional reasons. If someone who wants a just-for-fun shag takes advantage of someone who's after something more, it's mean, selfish and cheap — and the sex *won't* be great. Even if you can find a partner who also wants "no strings" sex, it might not be plain sailing. After all, you might be surprised to find that you get more attached to them than you'd planned, want to have a relationship, and be hurt when *you* get the brush-off.

MAKING GREAT SEX EVEN GREATER

Once you've got the right person and the right circumstances you're on the road to great sex. The longer you and your partner stay together, the better the sex will get. There's no mystery to this — it's because the better you get to know each other, the more you'll both know what the other likes.

There are two kinds of pleasure you can feel during sex. One is basic physical pleasure. The other is the satisfaction and pride of knowing that your partner is enjoying the whole thing as much as you are. It's like Christmas, really — if you got loads of fabulous presents, but suspected that all your friends and family didn't like the presents you'd given them, you'd be pretty miserable. The perfect Christmas would be one where you knew that everyone had loved your pressies as much as you liked yours, wouldn't it? Sex is the same. Here's what you can do to get that perfect balance:

• Finding out what your partner likes
First, look for clues. Does your partner seem to be having a good time? Are there some times during sex when they seem happier than others? Do they enjoy lots of foreplay before sex or do they just want to get on with it? Do they seem keen to cuddle and kiss during sex? Do they prefer a particular position? Do they want to try lots of different positions or just stick with one? Apart from just observing and guessing, it's helpful to ask questions occasionally. Of course, a full-blown interrogation during sex, or a kind of post-mortem afterwards would be rather horrible for both of you. Instead, you can just say, "Do you like it like this?" when you're bonking in a certain position or in a certain way (harder, softer, faster, slower). Or you could say, "Does this feel nice?" when you're touching, licking, nibbling, whatever. A good combination of observing, guessing and asking will help you get a really clear picture of everything your partner likes.

• Finding out what they don't like
This is just as important as what they *do* like, so always be alert for signs that your partner is feeling uncomfortable or would rather be doing something else. If you're trying something new for the first time (anything from ear-nibbling to talking dirty to oral sex)

and you're not sure if your partner is enjoying it, always ask early on. There's nothing worse for both of you than spending ages doing something that one of you doesn't like.

• Letting your partner know *your* likes and dislikes.
It's equally important that your partner gets to enjoy the same happy balance between giving and getting pleasure. Do everything you can to help. Don't be afraid to say, "That feels great!" or "I love it like this!" — it's flattering and encouraging as well as useful. Don't be afraid to give clues about the things you're not so keen on, either — your partner will be glad to know, not upset.

• Making compromises.
There are bound to be things that you adore and your partner doesn't, and vice versa. That doesn't have to mean that these things are out of the window. As long as neither of you ever forces the other into doing something they really hate, there's no reason why you shouldn't compromise now and again. Sometimes it's nice to do something even if only one of you likes it, because even the person who isn't so keen can get a lot of pleasure from knowing that it's making their partner happy.

MORE SECRETS OF GREAT SEX

There is one more very important thing to know: really great sex isn't just about bosoms and bums and willies and fannies. Because these bits are the most sensitive in a sexual way, many people ignore just about everything else. This can be a big mistake. There is so much other fabulous, exciting stuff you can do that doesn't involve the sexual "target" areas, and can make your partner go completely gooey. Here are some things that you may not have thought of doing, which loads of people absolutely adore:

- Snogging during sex
- Hugging during sex
- Having their hair stroked or played with
- Having their neck or ears nibbled, kissed, sucked, licked or nuzzled
- Having their back stroked or gently scratched
- Having their toes or fingers nibbled, kissed, sucked or licked
- Being told how gorgeous and sexy they are
- Talking about their fantasies

- Having romantic or dirty things whispered to them

...And there are many more. Use your imagination and never forget that you're having sex with a person, not a collection of body-parts.

Chapter Eight

PROBLEMS WITH SEX

The road to a happy sex life is full of potential problems and pitfalls. With a combination of sense and luck, you might manage to avoid them all. If you're careless or unlucky, you could come a cropper with more than your fair share.

Every problem has some kind of solution. The very worst thing you can do is ignore problems and hope that they'll go away all by themselves, because they hardly ever do. This chapter deals with all sorts of problems from the minor to the very serious. You'll find everything you need to know about solving them, avoiding them or — if the worst comes to the worst — picking yourself up and getting back on the road to happiness.

PHYSICAL PROBLEMS WITH SEX

These are the most common troubles...

Even when I'm excited, I find that my willy goes soft before I get a chance to use it...

Many boys, especially when they've first started being sexually active, find it hard to keep their erections. Usually things start off fine, then you go to put a condom on, or try to put your willy inside your partner, and bingo — it goes limp. It can be very upsetting and frustrating, but the worst thing you can do is drive yourself crazy worrying that there's something horribly wrong with you, because the whole thing is usually caused by worry and nervousness in the first place. You'll find that this problem can be overcome fairly easily, as long as your partner is kind and understanding, and you're prepared to try and relax. One practical solution that's worth a try is to grip and firmly squeeze the base of the willy while you're trying to put on the condom or enter your partner or whatever. Either you or your partner can do this, and it works by stopping the blood from rushing out of the willy, and therefore keeps it erect. If this doesn't work for you, just take a breather, then start cuddling, kissing and petting until your willy is hard again and have another go. If it takes a few tries, who cares? No one ever said that sex had to be quick and immediate to be fun! If you're unlucky enough to have an unsympathetic partner who seems impatient or disappointed, it's going to be much harder to overcome. It's worth talking to them about how pressurised and upset you feel. If they really can't understand, perhaps it's time to start looking for a new partner!

In the long term, this problem will probably disappear as you get older and more experienced (and therefore more relaxed). If it doesn't, it can mean that you're suffering from a condition called *impotence*. Sometimes there are physical reasons for this — such as a damaged blood vessel restricting the flow of blood into your willy and making it impossible for you to get a proper erection, or a problem with your hormones, caused by conditions like diabetes. The great news is that there are medical cures and solutions to impotence, so it's always worth visiting your GP or clinic. If the doctor can't find anything physically wrong, you can get referred to a sex therapist who can try and help you with the psychological side of things.

This problem can also be caused by drinking too much alcohol. It's called *Brewer's Droop*, and it's pretty common. Some boys and men find they can drink loads without it affecting their willy, others need only look at a half of cider and their tackle is out of action for the night — it all depends on how your body works. If you suspect this might be the root of your problem, try going without booze and see what happens.

I always come really quickly — like after only a few seconds. Sometimes I don't even manage to hold on until I get inside!

This problem is called *premature ejaculation*, and it's another one that's really common for boys who are just starting to have sex. You can usually put it down to nerves, and most boys find that it happens less and less as time goes on. However, some men continue to suffer from it throughout their lives. Again, an understanding partner is a big help, and there are plenty of things you can both try to sort things out. The simplest is just to relax a while, then start again. Some boys find that the solution is to have an orgasm deliberately before having sex (by wanking themselves off, or letting their partner wank them or give them a blow job). Either way, if you've already come once, it should be much easier to hold on longer the second time around. The most important thing is not to let yourself get into a panic — it'll definitely make things worse. If you don't normally suffer from premature ejaculation, but it happens on the off-chance, don't immediately assume that your partner is going to be disappointed by your "performance". Many people take their partner's speedy orgasm as a huge compliment — they could flatter themselves that you were *so* excited by the prospect of having sex with them that you couldn't control yourself!

Whatever your partner's attitude, they shouldn't have much reason to complain as long as you continue to cuddle and kiss them and give them lots of loving attention, rather than just rolling over and feeling sorry for yourself.

Every time I've tried to have sex, it's been impossible for my partner to get his willy inside me. What's wrong with me?

Usually this is just a case of everything being too dry, both of you feeling uncomfortable, and no one wanting to force anything too hard in case they hurt themselves or their partner. This can normally be sorted out by relaxing a bit more or doing foreplay stuff for a bit longer. Hopefully, this will make the girl produce her natural vaginal juices, which act as a brilliant lubricant and should help her partner's willy slip in easily and comfortably. Alternatively, you could take a short-cut and use some lubricant (for a reminder, flip back to the section about losing your virginity at the end of Chapter Four).

It's possible — though not as likely — that your problem isn't caused by a dry fanny but by something else. Another possibility is that at the point where your boyfriend is about to enter you, your vaginal muscles tighten up like crazy. It's very hard for a willy to go in when your fanny is virtually clamped shut! This is another problem caused by nerves, and, again, the answer is to try and chill out a bit. If you're tensing up because you're frightened that your partner's willy is going to hurt you as it goes in, you might find that you'd be more relaxed if you had more control over what was going on. The easiest way to do that is to have your partner lie on his back when his willy is hard, sit straddled over him, guide his willy to the right place, then gently lower yourself onto it. That way his willy goes in when *you're* ready, as slowly and gently as you want.

PROBLEMS AFTER SEX

If you use a condom when you have sex, you're fairly well-protected against getting pregnant or getting AIDS or any other STD. If you use some other form of contraception you're well protected against pregnancy, but not protected at all against diseases. If you don't use anything, or you use silly tricks which aren't actually methods of contraception at all (see Chapter Five), you're not protected against anything. You're also at risk if something goes wrong with your protection. And all sorts of things can go wrong... Your condom can break, leak or come off, you can forget your pill, your pill can fail to work because you're taking a certain kind of antibiotic medicine (always tell your doctor you're on the pill before he prescribes you anything), or your pill can get flushed out of your body before it has a chance to get absorbed if you throw up or get bad diarrhoea. Once you've had an accident, or taken a risk, it's too late to go back. But that doesn't mean you should just cross your fingers and hope that everything will be okay. Here's everything you need to know about damage control...

PREGNANCY

• A very useful thing to know: if you've had unprotected sex, you still have a chance of preventing a pregnancy, if you act quickly. There are special pills available for girls which are commonly known as *the morning-after pill*. You can take them up to 72 hours after unprotected sex, and they can stop you from getting pregnant.

This is also called *Emergency Contraception*, and your

doctor or a Family Planning Clinic should be able to tell you all about it and give you a prescription. The morning-after pill can be a real life-saver in an emergency, but it's important to know that it's *not* an alternative method of contraception: doctors don't like to let people use them more than once a year for health and safety reasons. You should also know that the morning-after pill can make you feel very sick, drowsy or dizzy, and could actually make you throw-up or pass out. Because of this, you should be prepared to take the day off work or school if you take it. Don't let these warnings put you off, though — compared to dealing with an unplanned pregnancy, it's a walk in the park.

The government is considering making the morning-after pill available over-the-counter in the future. This means that one day it might be possible to get it just by nipping into the chemist — or even to the supermarket or garage shop — and buying it, just like that. The most obvious problem with this idea is that it might encourage people to use it more often than they should, but it's certainly an interesting idea, and could help prevent a lot of unwanted pregnancies. Keep your eye on the newspapers for updates.

• There is another method of emergency contraception available. It's called the *Emergency IUD* or the *morning-after coil*, and it's the same sort of thing as the regular coil — a little metal and plastic device which a doctor fits into the entrance of your womb. If you get one fitted no later than five days after unprotected sex, it'll almost certainly stop you from getting pregnant, because even if an egg has been fertilized, it won't be able to settle in your womb, and will come out in your period instead. The problem is that the coil has quite a few drawbacks (flip back to Chapter Five if you've forgotten what they are), and doctors don't usually recommend it for young girls, or women who haven't had a baby. Still, if it's too late to use the morning-after pill, and you're desperate, your doctor might consider it worth the risk, so it's worth asking about it.

• If you're a boy and you have unprotected sex, you should talk to your girlfriend about getting emergency contraception — she might not know about it, or may have just decided to hope for the best. It's in your interest to persuade her to visit her doctor or a clinic — after all, a pregnancy would spell trouble for *you*, too. It would also be nice to offer to go with her for support and company.

• If you've had unprotected sex and you haven't used emergency contraception, you should start thinking immediately about the fact that you might be pregnant. Ignoring the possibility isn't going to make it go away, and the sooner you find out what the score is, the better. If you're not pregnant, you can breathe a sigh of relief and get on with your life. If you are, you'll have plenty of time to think it through. To find out whether you're pregnant or not, you'll need to have a pregnancy test. This means testing a sample of your wee or blood to look for pregnancy hormones. These usually appear around the time your next period is due. If you don't have regular periods, don't panic — let's just say we're talking about two or three weeks after you had unprotected sex. Although you should never delay getting a test done, beware of testing too early — you could get a negative result even if you *are* pregnant.

• You can get a pregnancy test done by a doctor, clinic or pharmacist, or do one yourself. If you chose DIY, you'll need to buy a home pregnancy testing kit. These are available over the counter from chemists, and they're easy to use, but not cheap. If you'd rather save your money, wee into a small, clean, dry container with a screw-on lid and take your sample to your GP or local Family Planning Clinic, where they'll do a test for you.

You should use the first wee you do in the morning, because it's been in your bladder longer, and will have more hormones in it if you're pregnant. A doctor may decide to do a blood-test instead of a urine-test, in which case he or she will take a little blood from your arm.

Your doctor should keep your visit secret if you ask him to, even if you're under 16. If you're really worried, you might prefer to see a clinic, where you're guaranteed confidentiality.

• You might come across adverts on posters and in magazines for "Pregnancy testing and advisory services". Although some of the organisations which place these ads are very helpful, others have hidden motives, and if it turns out that you are pregnant, might try to persuade you to do what *they* think is right. Some are very anti-abortion, and could try to put you off getting your pregnancy terminated. Others are actually private abortion specialists, and might try their best to persuade you to have an abortion with them — which could turn out to be expensive. If you decide to contact one of these services, don't let anyone talk you into anything you're not absolutely certain about. You've got to make up your own mind. We've put the numbers of some brilliantly helpful, unbiased agencies in the back of this book.

• If a pregnancy test is negative, you're almost definitely in the clear. If your period doesn't come in a couple of months, though, you should do another test, just to be sure — negative tests are occasionally wrong.

• If a pregnancy test is positive, it means you're pregnant — positive tests are almost never wrong.

• As soon as you find out that you're pregnant, you need to start thinking about the future right away — don't put it off until later. Visit your GP or a Family Planning Clinic as soon as you can, so that you can talk through your options, and get all the info you'll need to make up your mind about what to do. It's also much easier to think straight if you've got someone else to talk it all through with, especially an adult who can be rational. Many girls are surprised just how helpful and supportive their parents can be, even if they're shocked or annoyed at first. If you really can't talk to your parents, go to a friendly older relative, a nice teacher, or the school counsellor, if you're lucky enough to have one.

• Your options are fairly basic: you can have an abortion, you can go through with the pregnancy and then have the baby adopted, or you can keep the baby. It may also be possible for you to have the baby, have it fostered, then have it back when you're older, but this is far trickier and more stressful than it sounds, and may not be possible.

• If you're in a loving relationship, you will want to share all this horrible, difficult decision-making with your boyfriend. However, you should always have the final say, because whichever choice you make, *you* are going to be more directly affected than him.

HAVING AN ABORTION

• If you definitely don't want to have the baby at all, you'll need to go to a doctor or clinic, where they can sort out an abortion for you. If your doctor turns out to be very anti-abortion, go to a clinic instead.

• The sooner you see someone, the better, because the earlier you have an abortion, the less complicated it is medically. An early abortion (when you're less than fourteen weeks pregnant) involves a fairly simple operation where you have a local anaesthetic, and the foetus is gently sucked out with a special piece of equipment a bit like a mini-vacuum cleaner. The foetus is sometimes carefully scraped out instead of being sucked out. With both of these operations, you'll recover quite quickly — physically, anyway.

• A later abortion is a much more serious deal. You'll be taken into hospital and given hormones that will make your womb contract and push out the foetus. In other words, it's the same as giving birth, except that the baby is dead, and gets chucked away when it comes out. Physically, you'll feel groggy from the anti-pain drugs you'll be given, and take a while to recover. Emotionally, this kind of abortion is the most upsetting and difficult to cope with, although even an early abortion can leave you feeling sad, guilty or confused.

• The law says that it's illegal to abort a baby who would be technically considered capable of surviving outside the womb. If you are more than 28 weeks pregnant, you won't be allowed have an abortion for this reason. However, there is plenty of proof that even younger babies can survive with the right technology, so it's possible that the law could soon change to an even lower limit.

• Whatever you do, you should never try to abort yourself. Please take no notice if some prat tells you that you can get rid of a baby by throwing yourself downstairs, sitting in a hot bath, drinking gin, sticking a coat hanger up yourself or anything else. None of these methods work, and most of them are just stupidly dangerous. If you want to end a pregnancy, you'll need a proper abortion, performed by a doctor. There's no other choice.

HAVING THE BABY

• If you decide to go ahead and have the baby, you'll need to register with a doctor as soon as possible. He'll book a hospital for you, answer all your questions about the pregnancy, and arrange to see you regularly to check that all is well.

• If you decide that you want to have the baby adopted when it's born, you'll need to contact your Local Welfare office, which is part of the Social Services department. Your doctor or a counsellor might be able to help you do this, if you ask them. A care-worker there will make all the arrangements and tell you everything you need to know. Deciding to have your baby adopted is a very difficult decision. There's always the chance that after months of pregnancy, the amazing experience of birth, and actually seeing and holding your baby, you might not want to give it up. The good news is that you *can* change your mind once the baby is born. If you do decide to go through with the adoption, at least you can rest assured that you have made a childless couple very, very happy. Because adopting couples are so thoroughly checked out by the Social Services, you can also be sure that your baby will grow up in a wonderfully safe, nice loving home.

• It can be very tempting to keep the baby, even when your situation is far from ideal. Many girls who have less-than-happy home lives find it irresistible to imagine having a baby to love and care for, who would love them back. Others who feel under pressure to decide what they want to do with their lives see having a baby as a brilliant solution. And there are some girls who just love babies, and love the idea of motherhood. Whatever your reasons for wanting a baby, you should obviously be aware that this is probably the most important decision you'll ever make. The outcome is going to affect your whole life.

• Obviously the future will seem less daunting if your boyfriend turns out to be wonderfully caring and suggests getting married or moving in together so that you can share the responsibility of parenthood. However, even if this happens, you still need to think just as carefully about your decision. Babies aren't just about cute little clothes and lots of cuddles. They're expensive, they're hard work, and even if your parents or boyfriend have said that they're prepared to help out, at the end of the day being a mother is the biggest responsibility there is. Many girls go into motherhood young, and never regret it. Others feel like they've ruined their whole lives. The point is that you have to be 100 per cent sure that you know what you're getting into, because once you've got a baby, you can't send it back.

SEXUALLY TRANSMITTED DISEASES AND INFECTIONS

We've said lots so far about AIDS, but there are all sorts of other diseases you can pick up through having sex. These are called *Sexually Transmitted Diseases* (*STDs* for short), or *Venereal Diseases* (also known as *VD*). A slang term is *getting the clap*. You can even catch some things if you *are* using a condom, so it's definitely worth knowing what you're up against. These are the most common STDs:

CHLAMYDIA

This is the most common STD.

• You can get it from vaginal, anal or oral sex.

• How can you tell if you've got it? In males weeing is painful and there might be a thick, milky discharge from the willy. Often girls don't have any symptoms but you might bleed and find sex painful.

• How can you get rid of it? It can be treated with a course of medicine.

• What if you don't do anything about it? The infection can spread to other organs and lead to infertility.

GONORRHOEA

• You can get it from: vaginal, anal or oral sex.

• How can you tell if you've got it? Boys get pain when they're weeing and maybe a yellowy discharge from the willy. They sometimes also find their bum is itchy and uncomfortable and possibly has discharge. Girls sometimes have no symptoms at all, which is obviously a rather scary thought. Often the only clue a girl gets is if her partner develops symptoms. If a girl gets any herself, they'll appear within two to ten days of having sex, and can include: pain when weeing; a yellowy discharge from the fanny; a high temperature; feeling very cold; tummy ache; achy joints; itchy, uncomfortable bum, possibly with discharge.

• How can you get rid of it? It's easily cured with just one tablet.

• What if you don't do anything about it? The infection spreads to all your internal sex organs, causing pain and eventually damaging them so badly that you won't ever be able to make babies.

SYPHILIS

This is a particularly horrible infection.

• You can get it from: vaginal, anal or oral sex, and from rubbing your genitals against someone else's.

• How can you tell if you've got it? First, look out for a little area that looks sore, but doesn't actually hurt, turning up in your mouth, on your willy, testicles or vaginal lips, or up your bum or vagina (in which case you may not notice it so easily). Other signs are a copper-coloured rash anywhere on the body; a headache; a sore throat; a high temperature; swollen glands; hair falling out. The first symptoms of Syphilis usually appear between three and six weeks after having sex.

• How can you get rid of it? It's very easy and quick to cure with a course of injections.

• What if you don't do anything about it? It causes serious damage to your internal organs and you could end up blind, paralysed, brain-damaged or mentally-ill — and in untreated cases, dead.

Genital Herpes

This is a virus, a bit like the one that gives you cold-sores. Although it isn't dangerous to your health in the long term, it can be painful and embarrassing. It's also particularly depressing because there is no permanent cure for it.

• You can get it from: vaginal, anal or oral sex.

• How can you tell if you've got it? By little cracked or

open sores which look a lot like cold-sores, on or around your willy, vagina or bum.

• How can you get rid of it? A doctor or clinic can give you tablets or creams to help make the sores go away. Many people also swear by homeopathic treatments. However, you can never totally get rid of a virus — it will always be in your body. That means there's always a chance that the sores could come back sometime.

• What if you don't do anything about it? The sores usually go away eventually, but it pays to be aware of what you've got, because they're highly infectious for anyone you sleep with.

HEPATITIS B

This is a dangerous virus that affects your liver.

• You can get it from: vaginal, anal or oral sex and by sharing used needles for drugs, or any other contact with infected blood — all the same ways, in fact, that you catch HIV.

• How can you tell if you've got it? Symptoms can take between six and 26 weeks to show up. When they do, they usually include headaches, loss of appetite, a raised temperature, achy joints, feeling sick and abdominal tenderness. You could also be sick and have an itchy rash. After a few days you might develop jaundice - your skin goes a yellowy colour, your wee turns a dark colour, and your poo is light .

• How can you get rid of it? Hepetitis B can be very serious, and often means going to hospital.

•What if you don't do anything about it? Hepetitis B can cause extremely serious liver damage and can even kill you. It's very important to see a doctor as soon as you get any suspicious symptoms. Avoid all alcohol. If you feel at risk, you can be protected by vaccination.

Pubic Lice

Also called *crabs*, these are horrible, weeny little bugs which like living in pubic hair.

• You can get them from: any kind of close sexual contact with someone who's got them.

• How can you tell if you've got them? Preposterous itching between your legs; tiny little black specks (the crabs) and white blobs (their eggs) visible on the skin around your pubes.

• How can you get rid of them? By dousing them with a special chemical solution that's available from the chemist's — that's the only way. Once they're treated, you should make sure all your towels, sheets and clothes are washed really well — otherwise there could still be some crabs lurking there, ready to move back in!

• What if you don't do anything about it? Leaving them untreated isn't dangerous, but would drive you quite mad in no time at all, because once crabs have moved in, they get busy laying eggs and sucking your blood, which itches like nothing on earth.

Genital Warts

These warts are caused by a similar virus to the one which causes regular warts.

• You can get them from: vaginal and anal sex. However, you can also get genital warts without having sex, if you're unlucky enough to already have the wart virus in your body.

• How can you tell if you've got them? They're little bumps which may or may not be achy and sore, on your privates or bum.

• How can you get rid of them? Your doctor will paint a liquid on mild or single warts regularly. It can take quite a long time to get rid of them for good. If you've got a lot of warts or a very big one they can be zapped with a special electric current. If you have a wart on your willy it might be frozen off. Never use the stuff you get from the chemist's for normal warts. Like all viruses, though, once it's in your system, it's there for good — which means that the warts could re-appear at some point.

• What if you don't do anything about them? They'll probably just stay where they are — and anyone you have sex with could catch them.

Penis Infections

There are a few different infections that a boy can get in his urethra — the tube which leads from the end of the willy to the bladder.

• You can get them from: a germ picked up during sex, but you can also get them without sex.

• How can you tell if you've got one? Discharge from your willy; pain when you wee.

• How can you get rid of it? Most infections can easily be cured with antibiotic tablets.

• What if you don't do anything about it? It could get worse, do some damage, or spread to other organs and do damage there. Don't ignore it.

Vaginal Infections

There are loads of different types of infections that you can get in your vagina.
• You can get them from germs picked up during sex. However, it's equally common to get a vaginal infection

that isn't connected with sex. You can also get one from wiping your bum the wrong way (from back to front, towards your fanny), from putting in a tampon with dirty hands, as part of being ill or stressed-out, as a result of being on the pill or a number of other things.

• How can you tell if you've got one? Unusual discharge — it could be white and thick like cottage cheese, yellowy, greenish, greyish, foamy, and smell very yeasty, funny, sour or downright revolting; a terribly itchy feeling inside or around your fanny; pain or burning when you wee.

• How can you get rid of it? It depends on what kind of infection you've got. Treatments can include antibiotic tablets, creams you rub on and pessaries — big pills which you put inside your vagina. Your infection might turn out to be what's called a Yeast Infection, the most common of which is called *Thrush.* There are plenty of good natural cures you can try at home, including putting plain, BIO yoghurt in your vagina using a tampon, and washing yourself out with a mixture of vinegar and warm water. However it's always best to see a doctor or clinic first, because you might need prescribed medicines for your particular infection.

• What if you don't do anything about it? It could get worse and more serious. It could also spread to your internal organs.

Cystitis

Cystitis isn't actually a sexually transmitted disease, but you can get it as a result of having sex. It's a kind of inflammation of the bladder (the organ that deals with your wee).

• You can get it from: accidentally bruising your bladder during bonking. It can also happen if you hold your wee in for way too long, or if a vaginal infection spreads to your bladder.

• How can you tell if you've got it? If you're weeing more often than normal; feeling like you desperately need to wee all the time, even when you've just been; getting a painful, burning sensation when you wee.

• How can you get rid of it? A doctor can give you antibiotics, if you need them. Otherwise, you can take a short course of medication — sachets of powder that you dissolve in water and drink — that you buy over the counter at chemists. Drinking lots of water usually helps speed up your recovery, and sitting in a hot bath, holding a hot water-bottle or taking a couple of aspirin can help you deal with the symptoms until they go away. Many women also find homeopathic treatments very effective for cystitis.

• What if you don't do anything about it? The symptoms of cystitis can get worse very quickly, and are often utterly unbearable, so most people wouldn't *want* to ignore it. It should go away eventually, unless it was caused by an infection (rather than bruising or irritation). Ignoring an infection is never a good idea.

HOW CAN YOU AVOID STDs?

• A lot of people think that catching an STD is something that only happens to people who shag around a lot. This is, of course, rubbish. You only need to sleep with *one* person to catch an STD.

• While STDs aren't actually "caused" by being promiscuous, it obviously stands to reason that the fewer people you go to bed with, the fewer chances you get to catch anything.

• It's also important that the people you sleep with are faithful to you, or they could catch something from someone else and pass it on.

• Choose your partners carefully — obviously the more someone sleeps around, the more chance *they* have of being infected with something.

• If you're about to have sex, and you suddenly notice that your partner has a weird discharge coming out of them (or on their undies), a revolting smell around their privates or a funny lump, bump or sore in an intimate place, you'd be mad to take the risk of bonking them.

• Condoms (and Femidoms) protect against *some* STDs

— another good reason to use them.

WHAT TO DO IF YOU THINK YOU HAVE AN STD OR INFECTION

• Don't ignore it! STDs don't go away by themselves, and many can do you serious harm if they're not treated. Besides, if you don't sort things out, you'll be passing the STD on to whoever you sleep with — so you won't be very popular! There's nothing "shameful" about catching an STD, and there's really no need to be embarrassed or worried what other people will think, so you should never be put off doing something about it.

• What you need to do is find your nearest special STD clinic and get down there pronto. Once you're there, there's no need to feel ashamed or nervous because all the other patients are there for the same reason as you, and none of the doctors or nurses are going to be shocked or disgusted — they've seen it all before. STD clinics are usually friendly, helpful and discreet. You don't have to give your real name or any details about yourself if you don't want to, and no one else will ever know you've been there. You don't need an appointment or a referral from your GP (you don't even need to tell your GP you're going) and the whole thing is free. All in all, a visit to an STD clinic is not the big deal you might fear, so there is no excuse for not going.

• When you visit a clinic, you'll get to see a doctor, who will ask you a few questions about your symptoms and give you a bunch of tests. These will probably involve getting samples of your blood, wee and stuff from your genitals, but none of it should hurt or be too embarrassing.

• They will usually examine discharges on the spot and you will be given treatment on the same day.

• You arrange another visit to find out the definite results of the tests. These results almost always confirm what you've already been told.

• The doctor usually suggests that you get in touch with the person you think you caught the disease from, and anyone else you've slept with since, because they'll probably need treatment too, and may not have realised that they had anything wrong with them. No one will *make* you contact your sexual partners, but they'll encourage and help you — or even do it for you, if you want.

• Once you start your treatment, you should get better pretty quickly, but it's important that you don't have sex again until you're totally cured.

SOMETHING EVERY GIRL SHOULD KNOW...

Once you become sexually active — that is, you start

having sex — you should visit your doctor or a clinic every three to five years to get a special test done for cervical cancer. This test is sometimes called a *pap test*, or a *smear*, and it involves the doctor popping a little spatula into your fanny and rubbing it against your cervix (the entrance to your womb) to get a tiny sample of cells. This test shouldn't hurt at all, and it's very important not to avoid having it done, because cervical cancer can be successfully cured if you find out that you have it early enough.

WHEN YOU DON'T WANT SEX...

This book is about nice sex — sex between two people who like each other, and want to enjoy each other. Unfortunately, this is not the only kind of sex that exists. Sex can also happen when one person wants it and the other doesn't, but is forced into it. Here is what you should know:

Rape And Assault

• If someone forces someone else — by hurting them, threatening them or scaring them — to have sex when they don't want to, it's *rape*.
• Rape is illegal. The penalty for rape is usually a long prison sentence, and the maximum penalty is life imprisonment. Even an attempted rape can get someone

put away for a long time.

• If someone touches, squeezes or gropes someone else's crotch, bum, or bosoms when they don't want to be touched that way, it's called *indecent assault*. Like rape, it's illegal and serious. Forcing someone to perform oral sex also counts as indecent assault.

• For someone to be charged with rape or indecent assault, it has to be proven that you didn't give them permission to do whatever it was that they did. This doesn't mean that you need to have put up a big fight — you'd very likely have been scared to or unable to. As long as you said "No", or "Stop" at some point, that would legally be clear enough. If the rape was committed by someone that you obviously wouldn't have wanted to have sex with (like your father, or a total stranger) it probably wouldn't matter if you'd said nothing.

• There is no such thing as "asking for it". No one wants or deserves to be raped, whether they go out wearing a mini-skirt, low-cut top or tight clothes, dance sexily at a disco, chat a man up, "come on" to him or even go back to his place.

• Statistics show that you're as likely to be raped by someone you know as by a stranger.

• Date rape is a relatively new word, and means being raped by someone you've been out with. It is no less serious or nasty than being raped by someone you don't know. No matter what leads up to a rape, you should still have the same rights. If you go out with a boy, go back to his place and even snog him or have a petting session, you can still say no to sex. If someone won't take no for an answer and forces you into sex, it's always rape.

• If someone tries to rape you, try to use good judgement in deciding what to do. If your attacker seems nervous, you might be able to scare him off, or buy yourself enough time to run away by saying "No!" very firmly, screaming and shouting for help, or fighting with him. Never forget that your body is your own, and you have a right to be angry if someone tries to do something you don't want. Use those angry feelings against your attacker. If you can manage a really hard kick between his legs, it should put your attacker out of action for at least a few seconds – hopefully long enough for you to escape. However, if you're attacked by someone who has or might have a weapon, or who seems very violent, it can be far more sensible not to fight. Even if you have the physical disadvantage, you can still use your cunning. Some women have succeeded in putting off even violent attackers by pretending to be sick, spitting, laughing, swearing or saying they have an STD or AIDS.

• The best prevention against rape and assault is to avoid potentially dodgy situations. Don't walk around on your own in lonely places – it's never worth taking a shortcut if it means walking down an alley or across parkland alone, even during the day. If you're going out at night, always plan ahead how you're going to get home safely. If you have to walk alone at night, choose busy, well-lit streets even if it takes you longer to get home and always stay alert and keep looking around so you'll know right away if you're being followed. Choose the busiest carriages on trains, and sit near the driver on buses. Never accept a lift, go for a walk or go into a room alone with a boy or man unless you know him well and trust him 100 per cent.

• Many girls help themselves to feel less scared of being attacked by taking self-defence courses, or carrying a rape alarm — a little thing that fits in a pocket or handbag and makes an extremely loud noise when you press its button.

• If you are raped or assaulted, you should always report it to the police *right away*. They'll want you to visit the police station immediately and they'll pick you up if you can't get there alone. You'll probably want to have a good shower or bath and scrub yourself clean before you do anything else, but it's really important that you don't do it until you've seen the police, because you could wash away vital evidence. Don't change your clothes, either.

• At the station you'll be looked after by an officer who's the same sex as you and a police doctor will deal with any injuries you have, as well as getting samples of anything your attacker might have left on your body (like his semen from inside you, or his skin from under your nails if you scratched him). You'll be asked some questions about what happened and what your attacker was like. Once all that's done, you're free to go home, and the police will either arrange for someone to pick you up or take you themselves.

• Going to the police can seem very daunting, but try to remember that it's well worth being brave and going through with it. If your attacker gets caught and put away, it means that justice is done, and you might have saved others from going though the same horrible thing that you did. Be aware too that some men are very cocky about their prospects of getting away with rape, because they know that girls often don't want to report it. Do you really want to help rapists get more confident by confirming their beliefs?

Incest

This word means sex between members of the same immediate family — usually a dad and daughter, mum and son or brother and sister. Incest is illegal, mainly because if a girl got pregnant by someone she was closely related to, the baby would be likely to have something very wrong with it. Incest only covers close family — parents, grandparents, uncles, aunts, brothers, sisters and step-siblings. It's legal for cousins to have relationships and marry and okay for them to have kids — although there can still be risks.

Apart from incest between brothers and sisters (which isn't all that common) most incest is actually child-abuse – where a parent or step-parent sexually molests or rapes their child.

Sexual Abuse And Molestation

These are very serious crimes which carry heavy prison sentences, and yet the terrible, tragic fact is that millions of kids and teenagers are subjected to unwanted sexual attention from adults every year. What's really sad is that the people committing the crime are so often the people who are supposed to care for their victim – parents, step parents, adoptive parents, foster parents, relatives and trusted family friends. Sometimes adults get away with sexual abuse by using violence, but in most cases they rely on threats, or just take advantage of the power they have as adults. Some abusers try to convince their victims that what's going on is normal, or try to make their victim feel that they've somehow encouraged it. To be sexually abused by someone you want to love, trust and be protected by, is one of the saddest, most horrible and disturbing things that can happen to anyone. If it has happened to you, there are two things you *must* do. Firstly, you must understand that it's not your fault, and that *you* haven't done anything wrong at all. It's the person who abused you who should be feeling guilty, not you. Secondly, it's *essential* that you don't keep your abuse a secret. The only way to get over what has happened to you, and to get on with your life and start feeling happy again, is to talk it through with someone.

Abuse causes huge emotional damage, which is just as serious as physical damage. If you broke your leg, would you pretend it hadn't happened, try to hide it and hope it would get better? Of course not. Emotional damage needs just as much attention if you want it to heal, so don't delay getting it. If you're at school, and there's a teacher you like and trust, you can approach them and ask them to put you in touch with a counsellor. Perhaps your school or college has a counsellor you can go to directly. Alternatively, you can phone Childline and speak to a sympathetic, trained professional who can tell you everything you need to know, or just listen to you. Their number is in the back of this book, along with details of other organisations who can help you.

Whether you eventually decide to get the law involved or not is entirely up to you. It's a horrible, confusing decision to make, but it can wait, and you should never let it put you off sharing your problem with someone else. Talking is really the only way to get rid of all the horrible feelings and suffering you're going through. Don't let *anything* stop you from doing it.

SEX AND THE LAW

There are all sorts of laws covering what you are and aren't allowed to do. For instance:

• In England, Scotland and Wales, it's illegal for a girl under the age of 16 to have sex with a boy or man. In Northern Ireland she has to be 17, and in the Republic of Ireland, it's 18. This is called the age of consent.

• There's no age of consent for a boy who wants to have sex with a girl or woman, but...

• It's illegal for boys under the age of 18 to have anal sex, oral sex or any other sexual contact with another male.

• There's no official age of consent for girls who want to have sex with other girls.

• It's illegal for men and women — of any age — to have anal sex with one another.

• Any couple found getting up to any sort of hanky panky — beyond cuddling, kissing and light petting — in a public place can be charged with an offence called "Gross Indecency".

• A gay man spotted repeatedly trying to chat up other men in a public place can be done for an offence called "importuning" or "soliciting".

Confusing, eh? Here's what it all means in real terms...

• The police don't go snooping around peering into people's bedrooms hoping to arrest people for the offences we've been talking about. The laws normally only get used if someone decides that they want charges to be brought — usually either the underage person or their parents or guardians. However, the police can bring charges even if no one asks them to — so if you were very publicly having a relationship with someone underage, you could risk getting into trouble if someone else found out and decided to go to the police.

• A girl who has sex under the age of consent can't get into trouble with the law herself — it'll always be the boy she had sex with who takes the rap. If the boy is over 14, he can be charged with "unlawful sexual intercourse", but to be honest, he's unlikely to get into any trouble at all if he's under 17 and he and his girlfriend can prove that they both wanted to have sex. If he's over 17, though, he could be looking at a prison sentence.

• Although there's no age of consent for a boy to have sex with a girl, a much older girl could be charged with indecent assault if she gets up to anything sexual with a boy who's under 16. This usually only happens when the girl is *lots* older than the boy — i.e. a grown woman.

• Although there are no hard and fast laws about lesbian relationships, it would be the same deal as above if an older woman was found to have had sexual contact with a female who was underage.

• If you were wondering why there are no laws in

particular about lesbianism, it's because when the homosexuality laws were being passed, Queen Victoria wouldn't sign the act, as she simply refused to believe that any woman would ever get up to such stuff, and announced that as far as she was concerned, there was no such thing as a gay woman and therefore no laws were needed.

• Did you spot the very strange fact that although anal sex is legal for two blokes (as long as they're over 18) it's not legal for a bloke and a woman?! Yes, even if you're grown up, married and both perfectly happy about the idea, it's still not allowed. Having said that, couples who want to have anal sex go ahead and do it anyway, and don't get into any trouble. This law is normally used when a woman wants to prosecute her partner, or if she's been raped.

• It seems wildly unfair that the age of consent for gay males is older than it is for anyone else. The fact is that society has always been pretty unfair to gay men, and it wasn't so long ago that it was still illegal for two men to have a sexual relationship at all. Hopefully, the age of consent for gay males will soon be lowered to give them the same rights as everyone else. At the moment, though, a huge number of gay men ignore this law anyway and start having relationships as soon as they feel ready. If you have underage gay sex and get found out, either you, your partner or both could take the rap. If your partner was much older than you, he could be charged with indecent assault, even if you wanted to have sex with him. Both of you could be charged with "buggery" (anal sex).

• If you're a bloke, don't worry about being done for soliciting or importuning if you're just chatting to another bloke in a bar, cafe or other regular public place — you're not doing anything wrong and won't get into trouble. These charges are usually only used for guys who hang around in notorious gay "pick up" areas wanting casual sex. These places are usually public toilets or bits of parkland. If someone suggests that you go to one of these places, think carefully. Apart from the risk of being arrested, the only people you'll meet are those who want a quick shag for the hell of it — not people who are interested in being friends or having a relationship.

PROSTITUTION

Prostitution (also known as being *on the game*) is when someone gets paid for having sex, or oral sex or wanking someone off. Female prostitutes are sometimes called *tarts, prozzies, streetwalkers* or*working girls.* Young male prostitutes are often called *rent boys* and they usually get used by men, not women. You can certainly get in plenty of trouble with the law over prostitution, but frankly, if you're involved in this sad and seedy world, that's the least of your worries. Young people get drawn into prostitution for all sorts of tragic and desperate reasons — trouble at home, homelessness, lack of money, drug-addiction, being lonely. Going on the game can seem like a way out, but it's really a one way ticket to worse situations and an even bigger feeling of being trapped, helpless and out of control. When you work as a prostitute you are likely to be ripped off, taken advantage of and exploited. If you don't already have a drug habit, you're likely to end up with one, and it's also extremely likely that at some point you'll catch an STD, get robbed, get beaten up and get sexually assaulted. You've also got a bigger than average chance of being murdered. Even if you're enormously lucky and manage to avoid all that, you'll be emotionally screwed up for life. Never be tempted into prostitution — it's not a solution to anything. If you're already involved, get out. Fast. There *are* alternatives, and there are people who can help you get out and get your life back together. See addresses at the back of this book.

Chapter Nine

SOME OTHER STUFF YOU MIGHT HAVE HEARD ABOUT...

Learning about sex can be confusing. Just when you think you've got a pretty good handle on the whole affair, you can hear about something from a friend, on TV, in a movie or even in a pop song that you've never heard of and that sounds really, really weird. Here are some of those questions that many people would love to ask, but don't dare...

What's an aphrodisiac?

It's something that you eat, drink or smell, which supposedly makes you feel extra-sexy and madly keen to shag, as if by magic. You might have heard that foods like oysters, peaches and garlic are aphrodisiacs, or been told about strange things like powdered rhino horn and crushed beetles (called *Spanish Fly*), or scents that are supposed to drive the opposite sex wild, like musk and *Pheromones.* Sadly, there's no proof that any of these things work at all, so it's never worth wasting your time or money.

What is Pornography?

Pornography — *porno* or *porn* for short — is the word for films, books or magazines that show naked men or women posing in a deliberately sexy way, touching each other, or actually having sex. These films, books and mags are also described as *dirty*, *blue* or *mucky* and they're designed to get people sexually excited.

There are so many different opinions about pornography. Many males and a few females like to look at porn while they're masturbating, and some couples like to look at it together. Other people want to see it banned, or just feel that it's "wrong". Many believe that it's degrading to the people in the pictures and encourages people to see others as "sex objects". Some even believe that it encourages men to rape women, although there's not much evidence to support that theory — in some countries where pornography is totally legal and much more readily available, there are fewer cases of rape. Other people don't object to porn itself, but hate the way that the porn industry is run: with the models and actors usually paid a pittance (especially the women) and often persuaded or forced to do things they don't want to do, while the folk at the top of the ladder (who are often criminals) rake in tons of cash. There are still others who don't particularly like porn, but don't want to see it banned, because they believe that banning books, magazines or films is censorship, and censorship is bad, because people should have the freedom to look at whatever they want. As you can see, porn is a very confusing issue! At the end of the day, though, common sense should tell us:

- There's nothing wrong with looking at images of other people's bodies if it gives us pleasure.

- You're not hurting anyone else if you look at it in private (rather than, say, pinning a dirty picture in your locker where someone else could see it and get offended).

- You have got to be mature and intelligent enough to understand that although it's okay to look at people in porn mags as sexual objects (because that's what they got paid to be), you've got to treat the people in your day to day life with respect, kindness and equality.

- There's no need to worry about enjoying porn, as long as it doesn't take over your life to the extent where you'd rather have a wank over a pile of dirty mags than a loving sexual relationship.

A lot of female comedians make jokes about vibrators. What are they?
They're things that some women use to masturbate with. A vibrator is a little, plastic, battery-operated gadget that vibrates very, very fast and is usually vaguely willy shaped. This is odd, because few women

actually put vibrators inside them — they hold them against their clitoris area. Most women find that they can have an orgasm very easily this way, and sex therapists often recommend vibrators to women who have trouble having orgasms. Many women who want to try a vibrator but are too embarrassed to buy one, find that they can get a similar effect from an electric massager, the handle of an electric toothbrush or even the corner of a washing machine or spin dryer that's on full-throttle!

Vibrators are safe, harmless and fun to use. However, as mentioned back in the section about AIDS in Chapter Five, you shouldn't share a vibrator — or any other "sex toy" — with someone else.

What other kinds of sex toy are there?

A sex toy is basically any gadget designed to be used for fun during sex or masturbation. They're also sometimes called *marital aids* (presumably because they're supposed to help married couples enjoy themselves together) but you don't have to be married to use them! They include:

- *Dildoes* — Plastic willy-shaped things that you can put inside you. Some women like these but most prefer vibrators. Some men like putting them up their bums.

- *Love eggs* — Pairs of little plastic or metal balls that you put in your fanny, where they're supposed to jiggle around and feel nice. In actual fact, most women who try them agree that they do very little and are a waste of money!

• *Textured sheaths* — These are things that are worn over the willy like a condom, and they look a bit like condoms too, only they've got an unusual texture. Some have little bobbles all over them, others have funny, frilly "feeler" bits sticking out like some odd sea creature. The general idea is that they feel very exciting for the wearer's partner, but most people don't find them terribly effective, and they look pretty stupid on, so there's always the risk that you'll both end up getting the giggles instead of getting turned on! The real problem with them, though, is when people assume that because they look like a condom, they protect like one. In fact, they don't provide any reliable protection at all, so you should always wear a real condom underneath. By the way, these things are not to be confused with "ribbed" condoms, which are made by many reputable condom companies — look out for the word *ribbed* or *arouser* on the box. These condoms have a ridged surface that is supposed to feel extra-nice for the girl, but they give protection too. Rather than try a textured sheath, go for these.

• *Penile rings* — also known as cock rings, these are little tight bands of metal that men can slip down over their willy. The idea is that when the willy is erect, the ring fits extra-snugly, and the willy stays harder for longer, by stopping the blood from flowing out of it. These do work, but they can be dangerous if you leave them on for too long (more than about 20 to 30 minutes), or use them too often. This is because as well as stopping blood from flowing out of the willy, they also stop fresh blood and oxygen from flowing in — which could *seriously* damage your willy.

What is 69?

69 is the name for a popular position to have oral sex in, where both partners can suck and kiss each other's bits at the same time. Basically, you lie side-by-side or one on top of the other, but head-to-tail, so that both your mouths are level with each other's crotches. It probably got its name because if you did a drawing of two pin-men in this position, it would look a bit like the number 69! It's also sometimes called *Soixante-neuf* (pronounced *swa-sont nerf*) which is the French word for the number 69.

What's a multiple orgasm? Women's magazines seem to mention them quite a lot...

They certainly do! A multiple orgasm means coming more than once in a very short time (like a minute or two), and it's something that only girls can experience. What happens is that sometimes a girl can come, but carry on feeling as excited as she did before she came. If she or her partner carry on doing nice things, it's possible for her to come again right away — and so on.

If this happens to you, it's lovely, but no girl should feel cheated or worried if it never happens — it's not a big deal.

What's a G-spot?

It's another favourite subject of women's mags, and it's the name given to a particular bunch of nerve endings that can be found inside the vagina, a few inches up, on what's called the front wall (the side nearest to your tummy). It's named after the scientist who discovered it, Dr. Ernst Grafenberg. Some women find that it's super sensitive, and say that they can have an orgasm by stimulating it with their fingers or an object, or having their partner do it with their fingers or willy (this is easiest if you're having sex "doggie-style"). Other women can't find it for the life of them, and swear that it doesn't exist — and some sex experts agree with them. If it works for you — brilliant. If not, don't worry — like multiple orgasms, finding your G-spot certainly isn't the be-all and end-all of sex!

Do boys have a G-spot?

Not exactly, but many experts say that the most similar thing is the prostate gland. This can be found inside your bum, a couple of inches up, on the front wall (the side nearest your tummy), and it feels like a firm lump. Some boys like to put their finger or an object up their bum to stimulate it, or enjoy their partner doing it for them. Others don't like the idea or feeling of having anything up their bum for any reason. Like the G-spot, it's no big deal — so don't get paranoid about missing out if you can't find it, or don't want to.

I saw the film When Harry Met Sally, *where Meg Ryan pretends to have an orgasm in a restaurant to prove to her friend that girls can trick their partners into thinking they've come. Why would you want to do that?*
Many women fake orgasms, and they do it for all sorts of reasons — because they want to please their partner, because they're tired and they want to finish having sex, or just because it becomes a habit. Faking orgasms is fine now and again, but it can be silly to fake it all the time, because it means that the girl's partner will assume that she is perfectly happy with her sex-life. If she doesn't mind not having orgasms, it's fine, but if she secretly wishes she was having orgasms, and that she and her partner could try out a few new things that might help her to come, there's no way that her partner will ever know about it, is there? Plus, the longer a girl goes on faking it, the more upset her partner will be if she eventually comes clean.

So can't you tell if a girl is faking it?
As Meg Ryan demonstrated in the movie, some girls are very good actresses! However, boys can look for clues if they really want to know the truth. When a girl comes, her nipples go hard and stick out more — so if your partner's nipples are still soft and flattish after she's

apparently come, she might well have been only pretending. Many girls also get a flush of pinkish colour over their faces, necks and chests after coming — and you definitely can't fake that!

Can men fake orgasms?
Some do occasionally — for all the same reasons as women — but obviously it's much easier to get sussed out. If a boy hasn't really come, he won't ejaculate, and his girlfriend wouldn't have to be a super-detective to find out — if there's no spunk, there was almost definitely no orgasm.

What is it with handcuffs? I've seen people in films and on telly make out that they're something to do with sex...
Using handcuffs during sex is part of something called *bondage*. It's a kind of sexy game, where someone ties their partner's wrists or ankles together, or ties them to the bedposts before sex or foreplay. It's very common, and those who are into it find it dead exciting. Some people use handcuffs, others prefer rope, or something soft like a scarf or a pair of tights.

Bondage can sound terribly perverted, but there's really nothing wrong with it as long as both partners trust each other and are equally into the idea. The person who's tied up should always feel sure that their partner will quit the game right away and untie them if they change their mind at any time. If you don't know your partner well enough to be sure of that, then the game could be quite scary and threatening, and is best avoided.

Tabloid newspapers often write about "three-in-a-bed" scandals. What the dickens is all that about?
Sex is designed for two people. However, it's not unheard of for three — usually two women and a man, or two men and a woman — to all go to bed together. This is called having a *threesome*. Anything can go on in a threesome, in just about any combination you can imagine, and if everyone involved is equally comfortable and happy, they can all can have a lovely time. Problems often come if two of the partners are a couple, and one gets jealous of what their other half gets up to with the third person. That's why although many people fantasise about having a threesome, not that many actually try it.

Is a threesome the same as an orgy?
No. An orgy is when four or more people get together. They were very popular in ancient Roman times, and they were very debauched, excessive affairs where the wine would flow, tons of food would get scoffed, and the shagging would go on for days. These days, an orgy is more likely to be called *group sex*, be arranged by a bunch of bored, older couples, and take place in someone's living room — far less glamorous, eh?

The newspapers often talk about wife-swapping, too. Is that the same thing?
Not exactly the same. In group sex, the idea is that everyone gets intimate with everyone else — or at least a few different people. Wife-swapping is when two or more couples get together, pair off with each other, then go off separately to have sex before going home with their original partner. Again, it's usually older couples who do this, but — despite the name — they wouldn't necessarily be married couples.

What's S&M?
S&M stands for *Sadism and Masochism.* Sadism is when someone gets turned on by hurting people, and Masochism is when someone gets turned on by being hurt. S&M is the term given to what a sadist and a masochist get up to together. This is obviously a much dodgier area than bondage, which is normally a safe, loving act when it's done between two people who care about each other. With S&M, it's absolutely essential that both partners trust each other and set clear boundaries to prevent them from going too far. S&M isn't particularly common, but that still doesn't mean that there's anything wrong with it — if both partners feel safe with what they're up to, and they're getting pleasure from one another, then there's nothing terribly wrong about it.

My friend told me that Madonna's song "Hanky Panky" was about spanking. I can't understand that — she seemed to be saying she liked it!
Yes, *Hanky Panky* was about spanking, but not the kind that some kids get for punishment from their parents. Spanking can also be another sex game. Some people like the idea of being playfully — or even not so playfully — smacked on the bottom during sex. Others are very much into the idea of doing it, so if these people find themselves together, there's nothing wrong with it at all. Again, trust and setting boundaries are the keys to this game being safe and fun for both partners. Some people only like spanking or being spanked if it doesn't really hurt, others actually like the fact that a firm smack stings a bit. If you ever decide to try spanking, be sure that you and your partner are in agreement on this subject well before you start!

When I said that I liked water-sports, my friend started giggling and said that meant that I liked people weeing on me during sex! Surely people don't do that?
People do all sorts of things, and yes, weeing on each other *is* one of them! Your friend is also right that this can be called *water-sports*. It's not particularly common, but some people find it very exciting indeed. It's also not unheard of for people to enjoy pooing on each other, believe it or not! Obviously these practices are messy and a bit unhygienic, but if both partners are keen, no one else has the right to say they shouldn't do it.

I've heard people on TV make jokes about farmers having sex with sheep. Does this really go on?
Having sex with animals is called *bestiality*. It doesn't happen a lot, but it does happen, and not just with farmers, or just with sheep. Obviously, it's not acceptable or natural: it's unhygienic, probably not very nice for the animal and morally iffy, as the animal can't consent to sex! It's also illegal. People who shag animals are usually either mentally disturbed, or actors in dodgy porno films who are being paid to do it. Having said that, many, many people fantasise about having their privates licked by an animal, and some even like to imagine shagging, or being shagged by one. Remember that fantasies are harmless, and don't mean that you'd want them to happen in real life. Having said that, more people than you'd expect — usually teenagers — will admit to encouraging the family pet to lick their privates, or deliberately letting a dog nuzzle their crotch (as some dogs tend to do anyway!). If you fall into this category, don't beat yourself up about it, or worry that you're a fully fledged "pervert". For reasons of hygiene, it's best to avoid doing it again, but it's not such a terrible thing: do yourself a favour by putting it down to experience and forgetting all about it.

What is voyeurism?
It's when you get turned on by secretly watching other people doing something intimate — anything from getting undressed to having sex. Some voyeurs have perfectly normal sex lives and are happy to get their

kicks occasionally by persuading their partners to play games where they pretend they don't know they're being watched. If the partner doesn't mind doing this, it's harmless. Unfortunately, though, most voyeurs only like to do their viewing with real secrecy, and that's when you get *Peeping Toms* - people who sneak around, trying to get glimpses of their unsuspecting victims getting their kit off. This is a nasty, calculated invasion of other people's privacy, not to mention illegal. Many voyeurs find their habits start by accident (such as accidentally catching a glimpse through the window of a neighbour undressing), turn into a habit, then quickly become an obsession. If you're into voyeurism and worried about it, you can see a sex therapist or counsellor for help.

What is exhibitionism?

It's the opposite of voyeurism — it means someone who likes other people to look at their bodies or watch them in sexual situations. Some exhibitionists enjoy getting undressed, parading around nude or even touching themselves by a window, with the curtains open in the hopes that someone will see. Others get a kick from having sex in places where they might be seen. This is fairly harmless, although it's a bit unreasonable to assume that anyone actually *wants* to see them. Sure someone might be delighted to get a "free show", but someone else might get pretty offended or upset. If a policeman sees you, or you get reported to the police, you could be charged with *indecent exposure* (for displaying yourself) or *gross indecency* (for shagging in public).

The darker side of exhibitionism is when people — usually men — expose their privates or play with themselves in public. They're called *flashers*, and they're usually slightly sick in the head. Flashing is illegal, and although flashers rarely touch, threaten or hurt anyone, it can be very scary and upsetting to be on the receiving end. Having said that, if you're the victim of a flasher the best thing to do is turn around and run away. You should also always report a flasher to the police — or tell a parent or teacher who'll report it for you. Flashers need help, and they also need to be stopped from scaring anyone else, so never keep it to yourself.

I'm a boy who likes wearing outrageous clothes. The other day, someone called me a transvestite. What's that?

Transvestism means, literally, cross-dressing: wearing clothes that are typical of the opposite sex. A transvestite is someone who does this, and it doesn't sound like you're one — you choose to wear unusual clothes, not "girls'" clothes.

Transvestism is far more common in boys than in girls (perhaps because it's not considered weird for girls to wear "boys' clothes" anyway). A boy or man who is a transvestite usually feels comfy and happy when he dresses as a girl, and may also get sexually excited when he does it. Transvestites are usually straight, and don't actually want to *be* girls; they just get a kick — sexual or otherwise — from dressing up. Discovering that you're into cross-dressing can be horribly confusing, and transvestites usually suffer in silence and do their dressing up in secret. If you think you might be a transvestite and want to talk about it, check out the addresses section.

Are transsexuals the same as transvestites?

No, it's a totally different deal. Transsexuals are males (and sometimes females) who feel that they were born the wrong sex. They usually fancy people of the same sex as them, feel more comfortable in the clothes of the opposite sex, feel uncomfortable about their bodies and sexual organs, and wish that they actually *were* the opposite gender. Transsexuals usually feel confused and depressed, and some eventually decide that they'd like to have a *sex change*. The proper term for this is *gender reassignment*, and it's a long and difficult process, involving years of counselling.

Male transsexuals are given hormones which can make them grow breasts and make their voices less deep, and they can also have electrolysis to get rid of facial and chest hair. Eventually they can have surgery to remove their willy and balls, and create a sort of vagina.

Female transsexuals get hormones that can make their voices deeper and help them grow facial hair. They can also have surgery to create a sort of willy. Although most transexuals are aware of their feelings from a young age, doctors won't even consider gender reassignment until well into adulthood, but you *can* get counselling. Look in the addresses section for contacts.

What does the word frigid *mean?*
Some people use this word to describe a girl or woman who doesn't like or want to have sex, and men sometimes use it an insult — usually when a girl refuses to sleep with them! In the past it was thought that frigidity was an actual medical condition, but it's now known that there's no such thing — how much you want or like sex is just a matter of taste, and there's certainly nothing medically wrong with you if you're not so keen.

WHERE CAN I GET HELP?

Not everybody is lucky enough to have someone they can talk to. Even if you do, there are times when what you really need is advice and support from an expert who has all the answers and is used to listening and helping people. On the following pages, you'll find a list of all the most reliable, helpful organisations, their phone numbers, what exactly they can do for you, and anything else you need to know about them. You might want to copy some of them into your own address book in case you ever need them.

Never be afraid to use these numbers. They are there for anyone who wants to use them, so don't let anything put you off calling. Don't worry about confidentiality —

you don't have to give any details about yourself unless you want to. Don't worry either that your problem or question might be silly or trivial, or that you might be wasting someone's time. If something is troubling you, then it's not silly, and no one will ever tell you that it is. If you're plain scared of calling, just take a deep breath and dial — once you're through, the person who answers is sure to be friendly and will do everything they can to put you at your ease — it's part of their job. Always remember that you're in control. You can ask for as little or as much help as *you* want, and no one will ever push you into saying or doing anything you don't want.

A final note: please don't *ever* ring any of these numbers as a joke. It's not fair on the hardworking, caring people who work for these services (often for free), and you might be preventing someone who really needs help from getting through.

DIRECTORY OF USEFUL ADDRESSES

• *THE NATIONAL ADVISORY SERVICE ON AIDS*
Your call will be answered by a trained counsellor who's an expert on everything to do with *AIDS* and *HIV*. If you'd like some leaflets to read, you can ring their leaflet-line and ask to be sent some.

Both lines are open 24 hours a day, every day and calls are free from anywhere in England and Northern Ireland.

Help-line: (0800) 567 123
Leaflet line: (0800) 555 777

• *THE TERRENCE HIGGINS TRUST*
Your call will be answered by a trained counsellor who's an expert on everything to do with *AIDS* and *HIV*. As well as giving help over the phone, they can also arrange to send you leaflets.

Lines are open from midday until 10.00 pm every day.

Help-line: (071) 242 1010

• *THE LESBIAN AND GAY SWITCHBOARD*
Your call will be answered by a trained counsellor who is gay or lesbian. They'll be pleased to answer any

question about *AIDS* and *HIV*, as well as providing help, advice and support (or just a chance to have a chat) if you're *confused or lonely*. They also have plenty of information about other groups and organisations around the country, and will be glad to give you details of what's in your area.

Lines are open 24 hours a day, every day.

Help-line: (071) 837-7324

• *CHILDLINE*

This wonderful help-line isn't just for children — teenagers are welcome to call too. Your call will be answered by a friendly, understanding, trained counsellor, and you can talk about *any problem* you might have, including *sexual abuse* and other nasty experiences, worries about *sexuality*, *pregnancy* or *sexual health*, *depression* and *troubles at home or school*. They can provide support and advice, practical help, or just the chance to talk things through — it's up to you.

Lines are open 24 hours a day, every day, and calls are free from anywhere in Great Britain and Northern Ireland.

Help-line: (0800) 1111

• *CARELINE*

Your call will be answered by a friendly and understanding trained counsellor who can deal with *any* problem, from *sexual abuse* to worries about *sexuality*, *pregnancy* or *sexual health*, to *depression* or *troubles at home or school*. If you need practical help with your problem, the counsellor can also refer you on to an appropriate organisation, group or clinic or your area.

Lines are open every weekday from 10 in the morning 'til 2 in the afternoon, and then again from 7 in the evening until 10. Careline is hoping to have the lines open all day, from 10 'til 10, by the end of 1994.

Help-line: (081) 514 1177

• *THE NSPCC*

The National Society for the Prevention of Cruelty to Children runs a brilliant help-line for kids and teenagers. Their trained counsellors offer support, advice and practical help with any problem, but especially *sexual or physical abuse.*

Lines are open 24 hours a day, every day, and calls are free from anywhere in Great Britain and Northern Ireland.

Help-line: (0800) 800 500

• *YOUTH ACCESS*

If you think you might actually like to *see a counsellor face-to-face*, Youth Access is a great national organisation who can help. They run a referral service, which means that you call them, explain the general nature of your problem, and tell them whereabouts you live, and they put you in touch with an appropriate group or organisation in your area. If you don't want to phone them, you can write instead (enclosing a stamped, self-addressed envelope if you can) and they'll send you the information back in a letter.

The phone line is open during office hours, every weekday.

Referral service: (0533) 558 763

Address (for writing to — no visitors please):
Youth Access,
Magazine Business Centre,
11 Newarke Street,
Leicester LE1 5SS

• *BROOK ADVISORY*

If you need help arranging *contraception*, the *morning-after pill, pregnancy testing, pregnancy care* or an *abortion*, or you want help with any *sex-related* or *sexual health problem*, this excellent organisation can help. They run a referral service, which means that if you call them and explain what kind of help you want, they can put you in touch with your nearest Brook Advisory Clinic or other sexual health clinic for young people. They can also put you in touch with a counsellor in your area, if you like. It's all totally confidential (you don't have to give any personal details) and being under 16 isn't a problem.

The referral service line is open from 9 in the morning 'til 5 in the afternoon every weekday.

Brook also have a fantastic automated help-line. That means that instead of being answered by a person, your call is taken by a clever computer which plays a recorded message. If you've got a push-button phone, you can answer the computer's questions and get given the exact information and advice you want about all aspects of birth-control, pregnancy and abortion — and there's plenty for boys as well as girls.

The automated help-line is open 24 hours a day, every day.

Referral service: (071) 708 1234

Help-line: (071) 617 8000

• *THE FAMILY PLANNING ASSOCIATION*

This wonderful organisation runs a help-line and information service for people who want help arranging *contraception, the morning-after pill, pregnancy testing, pregnancy care* or an *abortion*, or help with any *sex-related* or *sexual health problem*. They can answer questions and give advice over the phone, arrange to send you leaflets and booklets, and put you in touch with your nearest NHS Family Planning Clinic for practical help. It's all totally confidential (you don't have to give any personal details) and being under 16 isn't a problem.

Lines are open between 10 in the morning and 3 in the afternoon, every weekday.

Help-line: (071) 636 7866

• *THE BRITISH PREGNANCY ADVISORY SERVICE*

This organisation runs a referral service for most aspects of *birth control*, but specialises in counselling and practical help with *abortions*. When you call, you'll be given details of your nearest B.P.A.S. clinic (there are 26 nationwide). The service is confidential, and it's okay if you're under 16. The clinics are private, which means that they charge fees, but they're pretty low.

The phone-line is open between 9 in the morning and

5 in the afternoon every weekday, and 9 'til 2 on Saturdays. It stays open 'til 7 on Tuesdays.
Referral service: (071) 222 0985

• *BRITISH AGENCIES FOR ADOPTION AND FOSTERING*
If you're *pregnant* and interested in finding out more about *having your baby adopted*, these are the people to get in touch with. If you call their main office, they'll be happy to have a quick chat, then put you in touch with your regional office, who can help you in more depth. If you'd like a leaflet to read, you can write to them — just enclose 60p, a stamped, self-addressed envelope, and a note asking to be sent the leaflet called "Single, pregnant and thinking about adoption".
Phone during office hours on any weekday.
Office phone: (071) 407 8800
Address (for writing to — no visitors, please):
11 Southwark Street,
London SE1 1RQ

• *GINGERBREAD (support groups for lone parents)*
If you're pregnant and planning to keep your baby and raise it without your partner, or if you're a *single parent* already, it's well worth contacting Gingerbread. They have hundreds of groups in England, Wales, Scotland and Ireland, so there's bound to be one near where you live, and joining one is a great opportunity to get help, advice and support. Gingerbread also run an advice line, where you can talk to a professional counsellor. To find your nearest group, call the main office for your part of the country between 9 and 5, any weekday. You

can also write, if you'd rather, and you'll be sent back details in a letter.

To speak to a counsellor, phone the England and Wales office (between 9 and 5) and ask to be put through to the advice line.

Main office, England/Wales:
(071) 240 0953
35 Wellington Street, London WC2E 7BN.
Main office, Scotland:
(041) 353 0953
Maryhill Community Centre,
304 Maryhill Road, Glasgow G20 7YE
Main office, Northern Ireland:
(0232) 231 417
169 University Street, Belfast BT7 1HR
Main Office, Republic of Ireland:
(0001) 71 02 91
29-30 Dame Street, Dublin

- *THE ASSOCIATION TO AID SEXUAL AND PERSONAL RELATIONSHIPS OF PEOPLE WITH A DISABILITY*

If you're *disabled*, or your partner is, and you'd like to talk through any sexual or relationship problems with a helpful, trained counsellor, you can ring this organisation. They also have a range of booklets they can send you.

The counsellors are available on Tuesdays and Thursdays from 10.30 until 1.30, and Wednesdays from 1.30 until 4.30. If you just want to be sent booklets, you can call at any time during office hours, every weekday.

Help-line and office number: (071) 607 8851

• *THE CHILDREN'S LEGAL CENTRE*

This organisation is run especially for kids and teenagers, and they have a very useful help-line, where an expert can answer questions on *the law* and *government policies*, as well as offering legal advice. You can also write to them.

Lines are open between 2 and 5, every weekday.
Help-line: (071) 359 6251
Address (for letters only — no visitors, please):
The Children's Legal Centre
20 Compton Terrace
London N1 2UN

Apart from all these numbers, you can find numbers for many useful services in your area by looking in your local phone book. For instance, you'll find:

• *THE SAMARITANS*

(Look under "S")
Counselling for people who are suicidal, depressed and lonely. Available 24 hours a day.

• *THE CITIZENS ADVICE BUREAU*

(Look under "C")
Advice, information and help with legal issues and the law. Available during office hours.

• *THE RAPE CRISIS CENTRE*

(Look under "R")
Counselling, support and practical advice for girls and women who have been raped or sexually assaulted. Available 24 hours a day.

INDEX